artists in their gardens

Valerie Easton | David Laskin

Photography by
Allan Mandell

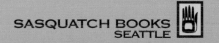
SASQUATCH BOOKS
SEATTLE

Page 1: A painted concrete cast of an exotic leaf from George Little and David Lewis. **Page 2:** Painters Grant Leier and Nixie Barton play exuberantly with color, texture, and structure in their Vancouver Island garden. **Opposite:** A serendipitous composition of foliage, pots, flowers, and a trademark concrete column in the garden of sculptors George Little and David Lewis. **Page 6:** Every horizontal surface in ceramicist Anne Hirondelle's studio is used to display the collections of natural objects that inspire her work. **Page 8:** A moist spot at Heronswood blooms with a colony of marsh orchids (*Dactyelorhiza*) overseen by the huge, umbrella-shaped leaves of *Darmera peltata.* **Page 160:** At Heronswood, the ancient, primeval feel of a Northwest forest is evoked by a half-sunken urn, as well as by the giant leaves of *Gunnera manicata* and *japonicus.*

Published by Sasquatch Books
Printed in Hong Kong
Distributed in Canada by Raincoast Books, Ltd.
08 07 06 05 04 03 02 01   7 6 5 4 3 2 1

Cover and interior design: Karen Schober
Copy editor: Alice Copp Smith

Library of Congress Cataloging in Publication Data
Easton, Valerie.
Artists in their gardens / Valerie Easton, David Laskin; photography by Allan Mandell.
p. cm.
ISBN 1-57061-244-7 (alk. paper)
1. Gardens. 2. Artists--homes and haunts. 3. Gardens--pictorial works. 4. Artists--homes and haunts--pictorial works. I. Laskin, David, 1953- II. Mandell, Allan. III. Title.

SB465.E28 2001
712'.6--dc21   00-049661

Sasquatch Books
615 Second Avenue
Seattle, Washington 98104
(206) 467-4300
www.SasquatchBooks.com
books@SasquatchBooks.com

For my mother, Barbara Singer, who made the garden in which I grew up. And for Greg, Katie, and Spencer, who have listened patiently to my stories and encouraged me in my mad pursuit of gardening.

—V. E.

For my friend Joyce Hartsfield, the artist in her own garden.

—D. L.

For my father, Hy Mandell, whose example as an artist has deeply inspired me.

—A. M.

contents

acknowledgments

First of all we want to thank all the artists who opened their gardens and studios to us, who shared their stories, secrets, histories and enthusiasms: Nixie Barton, Robert Bateman, Les Bugajski, Arthur Erickson, Dan Hinkley, Anne Hirondelle, Lee Kelly, Grant Leier, David Lewis, George Little, Johanna Nitzke Marquis, and Ginny Ruffner. We would also like to thank the artists' spouses and partners who were on hand (or in the background) to make our visits more pleasant and productive: Birgit Freybe Bateman, Robert Jones, Richard Marquis, and Bob Schwiesow.

Art is long, but life—and books—are short, and unfortunately we were unable to include in the final version of this book all the gardens we were privileged to see. We are especially grateful to Nancy Heckler and Mark Henry, who gave generously of their time for interviews, garden tours, and photography. Thanks also to Gathy Falk, Peter and Linda Fox, Thomas Gaff, and Lyn Noble in and around Vancouver, B.C., for sharing their gardens and the stories of how they came to make them. Alix Fischer and Kate Carson were most helpful at the Bateman garden, as were Cheryl Cooper and Barry Kaye at the Erickson garden.

Many thanks to Mark Kane for his insightful foreword, to Robert Irwin for the inspiration of his garden at the Getty Museum, and to Doug Bayley, Stephanie Feeney, Nancy Hammer, Paddy Wales, and the Pegasus Gallery on Saltspring Island for their knowledgeable suggestions. Thanks also to Rita Vincent for inspiration and generosity with her great ideas. We're also grateful to Martha Ferguson at the Miller Horticultural Library at the University of Washington.

We want most especially to thank Allan Mandell, who so beautifully captured on film the artists themselves, as well as the magic of their gardens.

Gary Luke, our editor at Sasquatch, and Karen Schober, the book's designer, brought their professional expertise, creativity, and precision to the project. Alice Smith did an exceptionally graceful copyedit. Thanks also to our agent Heide Lange for seeing the book through.

And last, but by no means least, we are grateful to our families for hanging in there through interminable drafts, laments, and exaltations about "our" artists and their amazing and sometimes far-flung gardens.

—*Valerie Easton and David Laskin*

Val and David have been first-class collaborators. Their complete trust in my eye and their solid upbeat attitude have been consistent from day one. They were a pair of white rabbits who invited me into a world I felt reluctant to leave. Some projects transform you as you work on them: spending time with the artists in their studios and gardens was to taste the fullness of lives lived with honesty, integrity, and a good sense of humor. Their courage is reflected in their work.

My gratitude also goes to the team at Sasquatch, to my friend Betsy Amster, and to my wife, Donatella, for her heartfelt support.

—*Allan Mandell*

Sculptor Lee Kelly's monolithic metal pieces serve as architecture in the garden, suggesting doors and windows between garden rooms.

foreword

Thank goodness for artists. They have to make art. They have to remake the world around them. Best of all (if you're a gardener), when artists catch the gardening bug, nothing they do is ordinary. Who sets a narrow yew in a sea of black mondo grass or puts carved heads in hollow logs scattered through the garden? Who introduces the garden that lies ahead with a pyramid of bowling balls along the driveway?

The rest of us, the fascinated spectators, reap the benefits. We come away from landscapes made by artists rich with ideas and renewed by a heady feeling of liberation. We're ready for daring. A sign in the garden of Grant Leier and Nixie Barton, who are among the artists in this book, sums up the lesson we take to heart, if we're lucky: "Be the Brave Gardener."

This book also solves a problem: Most of us have no chance to visit gardens made by artists (except in magazines). Once in awhile, the art museum or the garden club organizes a tour that includes the garden of an artist or two. Otherwise, could we find them? The answer is yes, here, in the pages of this book, which takes you to ten gardens made by artists, in tours of more depth than a magazine can offer.

The authors are qualified guides. An accomplished writer and gardener, Val Easton is also a librarian in the preeminent library for horticulturists and gardeners in Seattle, a preeminent city for gardening. She knows the gardens and gardeners, and grants us entrée to them. David Laskin, a writer who follows the bent of his curiosity—from weather to literary friendship to the wrangles of the New York intellectuals—became curious, and then obsessed, with gardens and gardeners soon after moving to Seattle. And so, naturally, he jumped at the chance to collaborate on this project.

Allan Mandell, the photographer, allows us to linger. He spent days in each garden, photographing most of them through several seasons, a rarity in garden photography, which typically shows a garden as it appeared to the camera during the course of one day.

Artists make having new ideas look easy. You and I stand amid the displays at the garden center and are overwhelmed by the variety of plants around us, unable to see that a hydrangea would fit that bare spot behind the hostas in the shade of the locust tree. The artist, thanks to training and talent, sees a simpler scene, made up not so much of plants but of shapes (upright, rounded, fan), colors that harmonize or contrast with one another (that silver leaf will nicely mute this vivid red), and textures composed by the size and arrangement of leaves (this carpet of thyme looks like velour, that holly looks as rough as a carpet made of jute). To artists, paths and arbors and plants are materials, like tubes of paint. An artist often launches into gardening and composes beautiful vistas of color and form before knowing the names of the plants. Les Bugajski's garden inspired the realization that the garden makes the gardener every bit as much as the gardener makes the garden. The rest of us can borrow a bit of the artist's training and an equal measure of willingness to act in spite of ignorance, to keep nudging and shaping until the picture looks right. As Arthur Erickson says, "I know when something is right, though I can't always give the reason."

The gardens on view in this book offer many rewards. Among the finest is companionship. Like the traditional arts, the gardens bring you close to the soul of another person, close enough that you feel the kinship linking all plucky people. You will also take away ideas. As Grant Leier and Nixie Barton do, why not pave paths with uncommon materials such as marbles, glass blocks, plastic fish, tiles? As Robert Bateman does, pay homage to the places you love best from your travels.

You're free to glean the ideas on your own or to rely on the authors, who single out some of the main elements of each garden and summarize them at the end of each garden profile. The sculpture garden of Lee Kelly inspires this comment (among others): "Color could easily be lost amid the plentiful green and brown of the garden—tree bark, needles, and leaves predominate, along with the stainless steel or rusted metal of the sculptures. So, when Kelly does use color, it is eye-catching. You won't find pastels or washy colors here—as they would just disappear."

You will also deepen your ability to understand gardens and apply what you learn to your own gardening. Not many of us think of our yards as a collection of volumes, but we all understand garden design in a new way when we see the four-foot high concrete head in Ginny Ruffner's garden and hear her say, "Any cube of space needs a center, a heart, an anchor, and in this case a muse." May your own muse inspire your gardening from now on.

—Mark Kane
Executive Garden Editor
Better Homes and Gardens

Left: "A garden without manipulation is really dull," proclaims painter Grant Leier, who collaborates on a never-dull garden with his wife, painter Nixie Barton.

Right: Ceramicist Anne Hirondelle punctuates a planting bed with a metal "spirit stick" by artist friend Russell Jaqua.

introduction

"I believe in the continuity and intrigue of all things—that comes from my art and extends to the garden," muses renowned glass artist Ginny Ruffner as she surveys a winged goddess statue exploding into bloom in her Seattle garden. She might be speaking for all twelve of the artists whose private, personal gardens are the subjects of this book. That gardening is an art is obvious to all who have a passion for making the earth bear beautiful things. But that artists—artists adept in nonhorticultural media, as opposed to landscape designers—practice this art with extraordinary results in their own backyards is perhaps less obvious. Yes, everyone knows about Monet's garden at Giverny, and a lot of noise was made over conceptual artist Robert Irwin's garden design for Southern California's Getty Center when it opened. But these gardens are considered to be uniquely aberrant crossings of creative currents. The truth is that scores of artists with a patch of ground and an itch to cultivate it are creating amazing gardens all around us: in tiny city backyards, behind fences, beside the sea, beneath dense stands of Douglas firs, on steep hillsides, in odd corners of commuter islands and semirural retreats, along busy urban streets and in ordinary suburban backyards. These are gardens that no conventional landscape designer would touch with a ten-foot pole: messy (or remarkably tidy), exuberant, quirky; full of mystery, strange objects, unheard-of plant combinations, undaunted experiments with scale, and flashes of pure originality in their approach and assumptions. Above all, these are gardens that reflect the creative temperaments of the artists who make them and live in them: painters, architects, sculptors, glass artists, multimedia artists, and, in one case, an artist whose medium is his garden—artists in all these areas share Ruffner's belief in "the continuity and intrigue of all things" and put that belief into practice on the earth and rocks surrounding their homes and studios. *Artists in Their Gardens*

presents profiles of twelve accomplished artists and the gardens they have made—or rather are in the continual process of making—for their own enjoyment.

As different as these artists are in character, aesthetic principles, station, and basic outlook on life, they have a number of ideas in common when it comes to gardening. First and perhaps most important is their *freshness*—in just about every sense of the word. Most of us, when confronted with a weed-choked lot we have just acquired as a package deal with our new home, think: clean it up, figure out where the hot spots and cool shady nooks are, pull up the plants we hate, put in some nice beds in harmonious colors and textures. But when sculptors and painters George Little and David Lewis took possession of a flat, featureless rectangle of ground on Bainbridge Island, they had the sheer audacity to make the place over to resemble an archaeological excavation site that would double as a showcase for their color-washed concrete columns and fountains. Canadian architect Arthur Erickson let the English cottage garden around his Vancouver house go completely wild for a couple of seasons, then bulldozed the whole thing, filled the resulting hole with water, planted bamboo and native grasses on the mound produced by the excavation, and let nature take its course. Renowned wildlife artist Robert Bateman had a vision that his Saltspring Island bluff could incorporate elements of Italian, Japanese, and West African peasant art yet retain its integrity as a maritime British Columbia ecosystem, and he set about transforming the property accordingly. Glass artist Ginny Ruffner expanded her home and studio to completely enclose her little urban garden, creating a sheltered microclimate in which to grow the fragrant vines she remembered from her Southern childhood. Lee Kelly created his own outdoor sculpture gallery by planting hundreds of trees on his rural Oregon acreage, fashioning a living canopy to lend scale to the giant metal forms he makes and displays there.

The point is, artists think differently. That's why we prize and pursue them. This "differentness" shows up most compellingly in their art—but it also surfaces in constantly surprising ways in their

gardens. And perhaps in quirkier, more intimate and more approachable ways in their personal gardens than in their "official" art. These artists' gardens are windows into the creative process, allowing us to see how finely tuned minds work (and play) with the juicy, prickly, fragrant, fragile, fussy, exuberant forms that spring from the ground around them.

Let's be honest. We wrote this book primarily because the two of us became fascinated by how many exquisite artists' gardens were growing in our part of the country—the mild maritime Pacific Northwest. But we also had our selfish reasons for launching into the endeavor. Both of us, as writers and as gardeners, wanted to be inspired by amazing gardens and the fascinating people who make them. We were curious to see what some of the Northwest's most eminent creative people were capable of doing with land in the same climate zone as ours. We were eager to immerse ourselves in artistic experimentation as applied to plants, hardscape, outdoor structures. Frankly, we wanted to see how much we could learn—and if possible crib for our own gardens—from gardeners who have a fresh, quirky take on planting and plants, light and texture, color and objects. Too often, we gardeners are plant lovers first and designers second—how many times have you walked around the garden, plastic nursery pot in hand, looking for a place to stick one more nursery find? We wanted to learn from artists who considered the big-picture possibilities of space, form, and scale first.

As we cast our nets and activated our networks, we looked for novelty, for the intuitive approach, for gardens unlike any we had seen before. We emerged from the project convinced that garden-making is not only a fine art, but by far the most challenging—and most mutable—of the arts. We became fascinated by the artistic process, by how a concept gets moved along from first germ to being worked out in soil, stone, and plants. In most cases, the advance planning and envisioning of the garden took place entirely in the artist's imagination. A few of our subjects admitted to making a hasty sketch, jotting down ideas in a notebook, staking out patterns on the ground—but for the most part these artists simply work from the unconscious, from that inexpressible but unshakable sense of rightness. We venture to say that the gardens we have written about are ten of the most spontaneous, free-form gardens to be found anywhere. Truly, they are gardens from the heart.

And, yes, we did find much to crib from and use in our own gardens. We share these tips in the sections titled "The Artist's Eye," included in each chapter. There we have collected everything from Robert Bateman's recipe for making naturalistic-looking artificial rock walls to Arthur Erickson's secrets for giving a long narrow lot the feel of generous flowing space to Dan Hinkley's formula for using plants as garden structure.

All of the personal gardens here offer glimpses of the innermost selves of the artists who created them; they share a common wellspring with the paintings, sculptures, pottery, collages, furniture, and buildings that the artists fashion—often in studios that are situated right in the gardens. But there is this fundamental difference between the gardens and the art created in them: the gardens are private. Unlike the art, the gardens are not intended for display, sale, criticism, or exhibition (with one exception—a metal sculptor whose works require the space of an outdoor gallery). The gardens are shrines to the muse and playgrounds for the artist: they are places to dabble, meditate, try out new textures and colors, worship, soak, laugh, eat, hang out, entertain—and of course plant, weed, and water. They are places, as they are for all gardeners, to get right down into the soil and get good and dirty. The gardens are in a sense the shadow side of the creative spirit—more akin to dreams, scrapbooks, doodles, to what the poet Robert Lowell calls "the wordless conscious" as opposed to "the uncomfortable full dress of words for print." But it is precisely because they are less deliberate, less public, less self-conscious and "full dress" than the "real" art that these gardens speak volumes about their creators as people, as artists, as members of family or community.

These gardens abound in qualities not commonly associated with gardening. Humor, for one. These are not always the most conventionally beautiful gardens (Heronswood is an exception, for it truly is one of the country's most ravishing gardens) and rarely are they the most immaculately maintained. They are buzzy, messy, tendrilly, productive, alive and enlivening outdoor spaces. Their boundaries are permeable; new plants, new ideas seep in, failures wither back into the soil. These artists admit, and even revel in, a realization most of us try to avoid—that garden-making is a process, one to be enjoyed with no thought of completion.

The artists' gardens are also surprisingly *useful*—again, a concept one doesn't usually associate with the private garden. Lee Kelly uses his acres outside Portland to display metal sculptures too immense for an indoor studio. Johanna Nitzke Marquis raises lush crops of potatoes alongside her roses and clematis. Dan Hinkley grows to mature perfection all of the plants he sells as four-inch babies at his nursery and through his famous catalogue. All the artists use their gardens as storehouses for cherished memories of places visited, friends loved, objects desired. They also use them as outdoor rooms in which to eat supper or drink tea, toss a frisbee for an energetic dog, curl up and read or sleep. These are gardens rich in association and rustling with inspiration.

Artists are notorious for being less than tidy, and in the garden this is a nice antidote to the neatness of suburbia and Martha Stewart compulsiveness. When a garden is constantly evolving, a work in progress, there is little time for fussing about perfect edging or neatly mowed lawn. Although suburban tidiness is not a priority, these gardens are uncommonly respectful of their sites, raw materials, topographic blessings and limitations. These artists show great ingenuity in making do with what is available. No time is wasted cruising the aisles of Home Depot in search of just the right piece of something. Instead they shape what they have at hand for another purpose that suits the inspiration of the moment.

Passion is the key. It's what artists have more of than ordinary mortals. The passion to take risks, go with their obsessions, and simply to be crazy because it's fun. Perhaps it is as much courage as passion—a courage to break the rules, to pay no attention to what

the neighbors may think. For all of these artists, passion makes the outlay of energy, time, money, and nerves worth it—an outlay they make on top of whatever they pour lavishly into their art. All of them approach their gardens with a vision, and whatever it takes to give their vision solidity in leaves and flowers, pots and structures they will happily do, season after season.

Because the creator and the garden are so intricately bound up together, we have made a special effort in the chapters that follow to include both verbal and photographic portraits of the artist-gardeners themselves—the element most often missing in garden books. In fact, getting to know so many exceptionally gifted (and generous) artists and to see how they have funneled their creative energy into the challenges of garden-making has been the most rewarding aspect of this book. These people, no matter what demands they faced in upcoming exhibitions, commissions to fill, images to seize on the wing, catalogues to write, weeds to pull, flowers to water, whole new borders to dream up, graciously welcomed us into their homes and studios, patiently answered our endless questions, posed for portraits, sweetly and enthusiastically encouraged us to follow them down yet another turn in the garden path that they themselves had taken a million times. These twelve artists are amazing people and inspiring gardeners, and both of us feel blessed for the hours we spent with them.

Some grave classical sage once said that the nature of art is both to delight and to instruct—and we can think of no better distillation of the essence of the gardens we have been privileged to write about in this book. Our intent has been to translate our pleasure and knowledge into words and images—to capture and cork at least a whiff of the strange and beguiling perfume that hovers over these gardens.

Dan Hinkley uses dirt, flowers, and foliage as the stuff of artistic expression at Heronswood, on Washington's Kitsap Peninsula.

Far left: The four-foot-high "Goddess of Beauty," with filigreed steel wings, serves as focal point and muse in Ruffner's garden.

Left: Nothing is ordinary or expected in this garden: a glass torso lights the way down a garden pathway.

The Continuity and Intrigue of All Things:
The Amazing Garden of Ginny Ruffner

Robert Louis Stevenson wrote a little poem for children entitled "Happy Thought" that consists of just two lines: "The world is so full of a number of things,/I'm sure we should all be as happy as kings." This simple expression could be the motivating principle behind the explosion of creativity, the marvel of inspiration, the glorious excessiveness of world-renowned glass artist Ginny Ruffner's multimedia art and her garden. Her aesthetic is one of appreciation, broad acceptance, and integration.

"I believe in the continuity and intrigue of all things—that comes from my art and extends to the garden," explains Ruffner. When asked which colors are her favorites, Ruffner explodes: "Bullshit—

I never met a color I didn't like! It depends on what a plant does—they're all different, just like people, just like a piece of art. How could I choose which color I like best? It's crazy—which finger do I like best? It's like in the book

Sophie's Choice—how to choose? I can't think of anything I don't like except maybe blackberry vines." Slugs? None have found their way into the warm, sheltered microclimate of her courtyard garden, enclosed on all four sides by fences and the brick walls of her home and studio.

Both Ruffner's art and her garden are celebrations of profusion—every color diffused into tints and hues, a mélange of motifs, a nurseryman's dream of plants, and a mind-boggling assemblage of media. "My whole life, all the space is filled—I have so much stuff it spilled out there," explains Ruffner of the eclectic mix of plants and art squeezed into her small garden. "I like to integrate objects of beauty with plants. People tend to view art in too precious a light, and maybe they don't view plants as precious enough."

Ruffner learned to love plants growing up in Atlanta, tutored by a gardening grandmother. "She could make anything grow," says Ruffner, "she was so Southern." Climbing roses, honeysuckle, and jasmine fill Ruffner's garden, twine about the gargantuan "Goddess of Beauty" sculpture, and climb up old brick to surround second-story windows and balconies. Their fragrance and lush textures create an oasis reminiscent of the Old South—transplanted to the mixed-use northwest Seattle neighborhood of taverns, car dealers, shops, residences, and restaurants known as "old Ballard."

This harking back to childhood plants must be the only thing the least bit old-fashioned about Ruffner. Her small frame topped by a tangle of bedroom-hair corkscrew curls in gold, red, and gray, she radiates energy and intelligence and purpose. She wears blue jeans, a paint-splotched black T-shirt, multicolored cat anklets and black sneakers fastened with the kind of spiral glitter laces usually reserved for four-year-old girls. You can count on dangly, funky earrings half-hidden by the pouf of hair. Ruffner earned a Master's in Fine Arts from the University of Georgia in 1975, moved to Seattle in 1984, and taught at the Pilchuck Glass School until 1991. In that year, her whirlwind of a life included the presidency of the Glass Art Society, curating a major glass show at the Tacoma Art Museum, and working as a member of the Seattle

Below: An orange begonia and *Hosta* 'Fire and Ice' mingle with the curling tendrils and fruit of a metal grapevine railing.

Right: Six rusty pergolas clad in roses enclose the garden's main pathway. The pale pink rose 'Cecile Brunner' climbs up to surround the studio's second-story windows.

Arts Commission and a trustee of the Pilchuck Glass School. She had three solo art exhibitions, and fourteen group shows, in museums from Japan to Michigan. Most amazingly, Ruffner and her assistants created about sixty new pieces of art, from glass sculptures to paintings and public art installations, some of which found their way into the hands of private collectors or into museums in Australia, Germany, Switzerland, and France, as well as the Smithsonian and the Metropolitan Museum among others here in the United States. That was the year 1991.

In 1992, Ruffner was involved in a head-on car accident while driving her parents' Thunderbird in North Carolina. The right half of her brain was severed from the left, and she was in a coma for five months. The doctors didn't expect her to recover. But her prodigious energy and will prevailed. Ruffner now walks again, albeit slowly, and though her speech is a bit painstaking, it is vivid with lively perspicacity. She recently finished a remodel of her home and studio, an old brick building that has grown organically ("It is always in a state of transformation," explains Ruffner) to more than 3,000 feet of working and living space that completely encloses the garden on two levels. Her energy and spirit are evident when she laughs about how guests at a housewarming party celebrating the completed remodel gave each other "body shots"— drinking tequila out of each other's navels. Ruffner's favorite housewarming gift was a basket of Barbie dolls with wild hairdos. The basket of naked, mop-topped Barbies now sits atop a bookcase holding *Redouté's Roses* as well as an eclectic mix of books on masks, shoes, shells, Botticelli, lace, textiles, sculpture, Currier & Ives. The collection provides clues to many motifs found in her garden and in her art: hands, grapes, vines, sumptuousness, shoes, the human heart, mystery, intrigue, romance, the buzz.

In 2000, Ruffner is again full of inspired plans and projects for the future. She is designing sets for Seattle Repertory Theatre's performance of *A Midsummer Night's Dream*, her first experience in theater design. "I love doing new things," Ruffner enthuses. "I'm going to emphasize magic and love." She is busy working toward a

one-woman show at the Seattle Art Museum late in the year that will celebrate the beauty and ephemeral nature of the garden. In preparation, her staff is drying millions of rose petals. For two years Ruffner collected all the petals from her own roses and spread them on countertops to dry. Then she realized she wasn't going to have enough petals, so she called around to "the big guys," and now local florists send her more than a thousand spent roses every Friday. Her studio is permeated with their fragrance, and every surface is slicked with a gloss of white, pink, and red. In addition, huge, flat styrofoam shapes dangling from the ceiling are coated with the petals. The shapes are reminiscent of mermaids, spirals, or maybe animal cookies, as humorously intriguing as creatures from the Dr. Seuss books. "I draw the shapes—I'm not sure what they are," explains Ruffner. "My assistants cut them out, we frost them with glue and then stick on the rose petals"—which they do by taking off their shoes and pressing the petals into the glue with their bare feet. Ruffner recently acquired a big barrel of a freeze drier, which produces more colorful petals than air-drying does. A sign on the freeze drier reads "Yes, I could dry pets. It takes 90 days to dry a dog—but, no, I won't do it." The plan for the show is that the petal-coated shapes will dangle from above, while the floor of the museum will be buried in petals, with pieces of art glass set amid the floral display. Ruffner's concept is to suggest the different degrees of preciousness found in shards of glass and rose petals: "Glass is precious and so are roses, but they are at opposite ends of the precious spectrum," she explains.

Ruffner's art often repeats the theme of containment, with elements such as glass balls displayed inside metal cages and bowls. She has brought this sense of enclosure to her garden, which started as an empty, weedy lot with a fence on two sides. In four years, she enlarged her building to two stories on three sides of the garden, with a solid, arbor-topped fence finishing off the fourth side. "In my house I love a feeling of—I wouldn't say safety,

The perfume of thousands of colorful rose petals laid out to dry permeates Ruffner's studio.

but coziness, of an embracing feeling, and you do that through scale," explains Ruffner. "We are 3-D objects in space, and this affects how we relate to what's around us." In the same way that the petal-encrusted shapes floating overhead in the studio emphasize the dimension of height and possibilities of space, so do the climbing vines and overhanging balconies emphasize the volume of space in the garden. A sweep of twisted, filigreed metal goes up an entire side of the building, serving as support for a lusty 'Cecile Brunner' rose that climbs to encircle second-story windows. A row of six rusty pergolas clothed in roses makes walking along a stone pathway an exercise in shade and sunlight, in fragrance and enclosure. A fluff of a tree fern spreads its elegant fronds, as lovely to look down on from the windows above as to sit beneath. Along the fence a raised bed holds arches of red 'Taboo' roses and blades of spiky iris. Rough-barked Douglas fir trunks ("It stopped traffic in Ballard when I had those delivered," laughs Ruffner) support the balconies that overhang the courtyard, which in turn hold pots of flowers and vines that trail down to the garden below.

Now all of this, with the scent of jasmine and roses filling the air, could evoke a charming Southern scene; but look a little closer and you'll get a whiff not so much of Charlestonian elegance but of the startlingly eccentric charm of the Savannah depicted in *Midnight in the Garden of Good and Evil.* In the center of the garden is the four-foot-high concrete head of Ruffner's "Goddess of Beauty" (purchased at a garden store), to which Ruffner has added huge steel wings that she describes as "weighing a ton, but not looking like they do." The wings are an elegant filigree of leaf, spiral, and other lively entwined shapes, curving out from the back of the goddess's head as if in preparation for flight. These same tendril-like shapes are repeated in the vines growing throughout the garden, in Ruffner's glass art, and, come to think of it, atop Ruffner's own curly head. "Any cube of space needs a center, a heart, an anchor, and in this case a muse," is how Ruffner explains the placement of her outsized goddess. And, of course, as with all else in the Ruffner aesthetic, the goddess is embellished to the max. A collar

Above: Ruffner's penchant for embellishment extends to a horned and jeweled skull that hangs above a doorway separating garden and living quarters.

Right: The orange bells of *Abutilon* and the spiky blades of yuccas thrive alongside glass balls in the warmth of Ruffner's sheltered courtyard garden.

of white impatiens frames her face, a fluffy hat of red impatiens is worthy of an Easter parade. As you stroll through this always-surprising garden, you are watched over by her brooding face, furthering the sense of safety and seclusion. It is just you and the goddess—and of course a riotous medley of colorful, fragrant plants, and perhaps the resident black-and-white cat, Studley.

In one corner of the garden a cushioned bench sits beneath a pergola nearly devoured by a honeysuckle vine. On a nearby table stands Ruffner's prize plant, a narrow, prickly crown-of-thorns, grown from a bit of a plant owned by her grandmother. This tiny

corner, nestled against brick and shielded by a scented vine, invites one to curl up with a book, sip a tall iced tea, bask in garden tradition. But what is seeping from beneath the nearby fence? A river of bubbles seems to be emerging, flowing across the stone patio, passing the pots of *Abutilon,* boxwood, and begonias to dribble down the black marble steps into the shade of the overhanging balconies. These flowing bubbles are actually a collection of glass balls crafted by Ruffner, some transparent, some translucent, arranged so that they grow smaller in size as they reach the lower levels of the garden.

The good horticulture going on in the garden, as well as some of the weirdness, is provided by Ben Hammontree, Ruffner's gardener, who lives in one of the second-story apartments overlooking the courtyard garden. "Ben is a Southern boy, too," explains Ruffner, "I love unusual plants, and he always brings me something new and odd—he likes the weird stuff." Hammontree is known in the Northwest for his "banana canna tropicana" style of gardening, and his hand can be spotted in the vibrant colors and the fatly bladed, striped 'Tropicana' cannas that embolden the garden. What chance could there be that two gardeners could be found who would share such an over-the-top aesthetic? Ruffner says it works because they share the garden. "We call it *our* garden—that's how I like to work," she points out. Perhaps this sharing of the task and the results is born of glass artistry, which is a communal venture, and of the fact that, as Ruffner is quick to point out, she accomplishes so much due to the help of her talented assistants.

"The garden is magic to me, and wonderfully amazing," marvels Ruffner. When she's asked if planning new plantings, or working or sitting in the garden, brings a respite from her art, Ruffner is astonished at the idea. "It would be like taking a respite from breathing," she exclaims. "The garden *is* art."

Right: Ginny Ruffner in her garden.

Far right: "My whole life, all the space is filled," says Ruffner of her eclectic aesthetic, which prevails indoors as well as out in the garden.

The Artist's Eye

Never Say No to Embellishment:
Marge Levy, director of the Pilchuck Glass School, once described Ruffner as having the intelligence of science mixed with the wackiness of a carnival. "When some people do something to excess, it can only look excessive. When Ginny does something to excess, it becomes glorious." Not content to leave undecorated the four-foot stone head that rises out of the center of the garden, Ruffner and her gardener, Ben Hammontree, devised a topiary-like framework to fit within the back of the hollow head. Planted with a cascade of flowers, it can suggest colorful hair, a hat, or a crown. A ruff of flowers surrounds the goddess's neck, suggesting a collar or a necklace; different years bring fuchsia, trailing ivy, impatiens, or begonias to the mix. Little topiaries on either side of her head give the illusion of drop earrings. A massive water buffalo skull with horns, mounted on the wall opposite the goddess, is itself ornamented with glass jewels.

The Art of Illusion:
Ruffner loves to trick, to cleverly fool, the eye with contrast and illusion. A brochure from an artists' series, published by a local winery, describes the intrigue of her glass this way: "The different surface media are manipulated to achieve a range of qualities from transparent through translucence to opacity." Ruffner plays with the surfaces and solidities of the garden as well. The glass "bubble" balls range from milky to transparent to cloudy, as if they mirrored the changing sky above. The heavy steel wings that surround the goddess's head are clearly metal, but their feel is nearly transparent, and this airiness is heightened by the flickers of bright impatiens planted to be glimpsed through the wings. Their filigreed texture, in contrast to their solid material, suggests that they are light as air—about to take flight and lift the huge head up to hover above the garden.

Movement and Momentum:
Both a work of art and a garden may appear static, frozen in time, but not in the Ruffner aesthetic. Not only humor but momentum is suggested by her art piece titled *Another Way for the Chicken to Cross the Road* (1994), which consists of a spotted hen atop what resembles a roller-derby car propelled along by two poles worked by a winged figure in striped tights. In the garden, this same momentum (and tweak of humor) comes from the stream of glass balls, resembling bubbles, that pop out from under the fence and make their dribbling way across a patio and down the steps. Each ball, of course, remains where it has been placed, amid foliage or lying in the corner of a glossy marble stair, but the feeling is of a river of bubbles emerging from an unseen source behind the fence and flowing through the garden. A grand steel trellis arch, 16 feet high by 14 feet wide, swoops along the north wall, its spirals and curling tendrils directing the eye along the side of the building, echoing the energy of the 'Cecile Brunner' rose that clambers along it. People, too, become part of the planned momentum of the garden; Ruffner makes her point that humans are 3-D objects moving through space by lining a stone pathway with a series of six rusted arbors, draped in roses. The effect is to gently direct the garden visitor through a tunnel of floral fragrance.

Melding Indoor and Outdoor Spaces:
With her love of the frenetic and eclectic, Ruffner makes indoor and outdoor spaces flow seamlessly together. Both studio and living space are oriented to the interior courtyard by large windows and glass sliders in the ground-floor rooms and on the second story. The garden is designed to be looked down upon from windows and balconies, and it is stretched up to bring fragrance, flower, and foliage to the upstairs by the roses that climb along trellis and wires surrounding second-story windows. The sitting room, which opens to the garden, continues the garden theme with plants in terra-cotta pots that echo outdoor containers, along with botanical prints and flowered upholstery. Funky pillows, a colorful checked floor, and spiral posts flanking a fireplace with a plant-bedecked mantel, as well as the light pouring in through the large windows, give the feeling of a garden room. Indoor comfort and repose is extended into the garden with cushioned benches and chairs lining balconies, fitting snugly beneath the overhangs, or tucked into vine-covered pergolas.

Far left: Anne Hirondelle's studio looks out to the garden through a pruned-up Japanese black pine. Touchstones collected from nature line shelves and windowsills.

Left: *Libertia grandiflora* in a Hirondelle-crafted vessel.

Spatial Compositions:
The Garden Rooms of Ceramicist Anne Hirondelle

The shelves in ceramic artist Anne Hirondelle's studio hold tidy rows and clusters of feathers, stones, tiny bird skeletons, nests, pods, and cones. Their colors and forms are touchstones for Hirondelle's art, as they were for another artist who collected skulls, rocks, bones, and feathers, Georgia O'Keeffe. The voluptuous, dreamlike imagery of O'Keeffe's paintings couldn't be more distant aesthetically from the subtle, traditional clay vessels crafted by Anne Hirondelle, nor could the two artists'

Below: Inspiration for both the color and texture of Hirondelle's ceramic work comes directly from nature, as in these bark-textured, gourd-like pots.

Right: The long graceful spurs of *Aquilegia* 'Olympia' accent the bristly needles of the pine in this textural composition.

Far right: A ceramic vessel set in the center of the Zen garden echoes the color, line, and papery texture of the surrounding birch trunks.

backgrounds be more different. O'Keeffe was born in the Midwest and spent her later life in her beloved New Mexican desert; Hirondelle grew up in western Oregon and now lives less than a mile from the sea, in Port Townsend, on Washington's Olympic Peninsula. Yet for both, the artistic impulse flows from the poetry inherent in natural

objects, and the simplicity and purity of these forms are expressed in both women's art, as well as in Hirondelle's garden.

"It is only by selection, by elimination, by emphasis that we get at the real meaning of things," said O'Keeffe in 1922. Hirondelle has created a hushed, calm, Zen-like oasis of a garden by just such ruthless elimination of anything that doesn't match her strong, simple aesthetic. In her elegantly composed garden, warmed by the onshore flow of moist air from nearby Puget Sound, plants have been selected with as much care as the objects on her studio shelves. Bright colors, showy forms, vivid ornamentation, flash, dash—all these have been avoided in the garden as well as in the studio. Colors are pared down to the subtle and natural, form is pure and sculptural. Richness comes not from elaboration or decoration but from the atmosphere of spaces contained, separate yet flowing. Hirondelle has created a series of garden rooms by dividing space into separate compartments as surely as the molded walls of her ceramic vessels divide space into two distinct parts—volume contained and space remaining outside.

Dividing a garden into rooms with brick walls and solid hedging is a familiar British concept. But such scale and grandeur would be inappropriate to a garden in quaint Port Townsend, so Hirondelle has adopted the concept with a twist. She has cleverly enlarged the spaces of her garden by allowing them to spill out visually from behind hedges, between trees and fences; rather than creating solid barriers, she suggests separation to create distinct atmospheres. A split-rail fence stretches across the grass, but stops short of the edges. You can walk right around the end of the fence as well as see through it. Hirondelle uses this familiar form merely to suggest the division of space. A small grove of birches creates a vertical pattern of white-dappled trunks and a horizontal pattern of shade upon grass. The result of such simple manipulations of space is a garden so full of serenity, so hushed and still, that even a black lab, that most rambunctious of dogs, would feel compelled to pause in his mad dash beneath the vine-draped entry pergola and put each paw down slowly and carefully as he soaked up the tranquillity.

This tranquillity is created in part because of the near-perfection of every plant and every object. Each looks as if Hirondelle had deliberately selected it just for that spot: the lilies, euphorbias, and azaleas thrive unshouldered by their neighbors, the little birch trees have plenty of room to grow to full size and their natural shape. "When I choose plants it is like everything else—I just choose what I like and then everything goes together okay because I like it." This philosophy is as deceptively simple as the garden itself, which is straightforward in its forms (mossy fence, hedges, old orchard, birch grove) but complex in emotional resonance. Hirondelle's garden is a place to linger, perhaps take a nap in the little grove of birches, or to pass through the gap in the fence on an Alice-in-Wonderland quest, just to see where it might lead. The fact that the lawn only leads around the corner to the old front porch dilutes the impact of the journey not a bit; it is the chance to pass through that archetypal form, open yet puzzling, that entices and enchants.

Economical of gesture and soft of voice, Hirondelle has a self-possessed, thoughtful manner perhaps bred of solitary hours in the studio and the garden. Her unruffled, shiny cap of silver-gray hair cleanly outlines her small face and wide smile. She wears tidy overalls and T-shirts, in the same subdued grays and browns of the wasp nests and pine cones she collects. You'd never take her for a woman who once aspired to become an attorney. Years ago, Hirondelle remarked to a friend, "I'm either going to law school or I'm going to make pots." Her

Below: An oriental poppy shares the glossy foliage of a *Bergenia*.

Right: *Iris pallida* 'Aurea Variegata' presents a pleasing counterpoint to the smooth, round shapes of a trio of bowls set out to hold rainwater.

friend responded, "Remember, you can always eat out of pots." Hirondelle had degrees in English and counseling psychology, she'd directed a social agency in Seattle, and then in the early '70s, she had decided to go to law school. The first day she knew she'd made a mistake, but she stuck it out for a year anyway, and then quit to begin taking ceramics classes. She had always been drawn to clay's plasticity, its mutability. Then, as now, what intrigued her was creating shape and form from clay rather than adding decoration to the pots. Neither does she decorate her garden.

Examine the teapot. Hirondelle uses the traditional rounded, handled shape of a teapot for its symbolic function; her goal is to create forms that appear full, perhaps overflowing, with memories or sensations. "A teapot need not be full of tea to communicate the spirit or ritual of tea," she says. Vessels are the core metaphor in her ceramics, used as a visual link between the past and future. Her ceramic vessels, slightly oversized pieces derived from the forms of traditional functional pots, play with the shaping of space. Uptilted handles or the thrust of a spout are the only elements that disrupt the simple curves of the sensual vessels. Surfaces are bronze, gray, or deep brown. She started by working with a variety of glazes, and now her work has evolved into architectural pieces that are exercises in pure form.

When Hirondelle and her husband, Bob Schwiesow, bought their old (circa 1902) farmhouse in a field on the Olympic Peninsula twenty years ago, the garden consisted of a cyclone fence and a vegetable garden with a cherry tree planted right in the center. It is an old garden, flat and grassy, the size of two city lots, in a neighborhood of small houses and big yards. Hirondelle began gardening to create some order, to bring a sense of passage and purpose to the space. She divided the lot into loosely defined "rooms" to make comfortable people-sized dimensions; there's an entry garden, a Zen garden, an orchard, a dining area. Attention to detail, shape, and form distinguishes her garden as it does her ceramic art. Vessels line her studio shelves, each pure in form and plump with volume, one a bit more glossy, another bumpier. The colors are of the earth, subdued studies in brown, cream, and gray. It is not surface decoration or ornamentation that characterize Hirondelle's ceramics, but natural textures and strong sculptural forms. This aesthetic continues out into the garden, where you'll find nary a showy dahlia or gazing globe; instead, it's a pine tree limbed up to reveal the curve of its trunk, the swell of a rounded *Rodgersia* leaf, or the curve of a pot set amidst a flower bed that catches the eye, creates the Zen-like atmosphere that draws a visitor into the meditative mood.

Hirondelle quotes poet Stanley Kunitz to explain the importance of gardening in her life. "Gardening for me is the passionate effort to organize a little corner of the earth, which I want to redeem. The wish is to achieve control over your little plot so that it appears beautiful, distinguished—an equivalent of your signature in the natural world." That sensibility is apparent in the well-cared-for feel of Hirondelle's garden, its affinity with the house and the studio, the restful feeling of all-of-a-piece work and thought that permeate all three. Even the cakes of Lifebuoy soap that hang from tree branches to ward away marauding deer look like tiny presents, each one carefully wrapped and tied as if for a children's party.

Her garden, she says, continues to be an antidote to too much clay. Anne took the name "Hirondelle," the French word for "swallow," in a symbolic effort to acquire strong wings. Yet each time she begins a new cycle of ceramic work, sketching new forms and translating them into three-dimensional clay, she feels the need for strength. "My small wings feel heavy with dust," she says. It is working in the soil, planting, refining, arranging exterior space and form, that renews her for her ceramic work.

What Hirondelle describes as her "overwhelming need to order things visually—a three-dimensional ordering" is satisfied in the garden as well as at her potting wheel. This sense of controlling and ordering space, as well as Hirondelle's strong aesthetic preference for the simple and unpretentious, has determined the design and content of the garden. She is drawn to the structure of plants, choosing

Above: A corner of the studio houses Hirondelle's collection of feathers, stones, and pods. Their subdued and subtle colors are reflected in her ceramics.

Right: Hirondelle uses the traditional shape of a teapot, slightly oversized, to conjure up the spirit and ritual of tea.

them for their line and architectural qualities. "I don't care what color they are," she explains, "I just want the leaf." It is very difficult for someone who loves plants to refine choices, to select just a few plants. Hirondelle's ability to pare down to form, to edit, to clearly see each individual element, has allowed her to create a garden of restful open spaces, devoid of overcrowding. Then, too, her precise planting is a result of limited funds: she has needed to wait to divide plants, and to buy trees and shrubs in small sizes.

Although her vessels begin with sketches on paper, she has never drawn plans for her garden, preferring to work it out in the dirt as

she goes along. Hirondelle considers not only the space within her garden, but also the space beyond it, taking advantage of the Japanese concept of "borrowed scenery." She prunes an old laurel hedge straight across, just high enough so that it echoes the brick wall of the neighbor's house, forming a pleasing contrast of color and texture. As one looks across the lawn, the eye is drawn into a clear horizontal rhythm of long, low, mossy fences, followed by the higher green hedge, and beyond that a clipped row of red-leafed 'Thundercloud' plum trees. There is superb geometry hidden within

Left: The Zen garden, with the orchard in the distance, as viewed through the spires of Jerusalem sage (*Phlomis russeliana*) and silvery lambs' ears (*Stachys byzantina*).

Below: Hirondelle planned a bed of peonies, iris, lambs' ears, and Spanish lavender around a ceramic vessel she received as a gift.

Above: Anne Hirondelle at work in her garden studio.

Right: A clipped boxwood hedge sets off the gently curved silhouette of a tall ceramic vessel and the pale pink fluffs of chenille-like *Polygonum bistorta* 'Superbum'.

the softness of the plantings. The forms of fence, hedge, and trees are simple and distinct, varying in texture and color, graduated in height, and repetitious in clean horizontal line.

In an artist's version of the Southern tradition of "pass-along" plants, Hirondelle has traded what she makes for what she can't afford to buy, enjoying the chance to display the metal and ceramic work of other artists that she admires. She collects large ceramic vessels that she sets amidst the plantings, all as subtly colored as if they had grown up from the ground; beige, brown, soft gray, with muted finishes and crackled or rough textures. A dark metal "spirit stick" by artist friend Russell Jaqua punctuates a planting of azaleas and boxwood. Even her light-filled studio, set into the garden, was acquired through trade. Jim Cutler, the Bainbridge Island architect famous for designing Bill Gates's vast home compound on Lake Washington, offered to design the studio he'd heard she wanted in exchange for several pieces of her work. Hirondelle demurred, saying she needed something small and simple enough for her husband to build himself. Cutler persisted, designing a studio that Schwiesow was able to build. It is a beautiful little pitched-roofed wooden structure, with paned windows, deep windowsills, and plenty of light. Here Hirondelle sketches, throws, and fires her ceramics, displays the natural objects from which she derives inspiration, and looks out upon the garden as she works.

"Through my vessels," says Hirondelle, "I hope to speak, not center stage, but in the quiet, contemplative niches and corners of the individual and collective psyche." In the garden she has created simple, soothing spaces that resonate with life and meaning: she has bestowed context by using the familiar forms of fence and hedge that refer to the age of the house and neighborhood. The garden is sufficiently simple and quiet in color to welcome the sumptuous silhouettes of the ceramic vessels placed precisely amongst the plantings. Most uniquely, she has manipulated form and space to create a garden of atmosphere and mood and even wonder. Swiss novelist Max Frisch talked about "the knack of so arranging the world that we don't have to experience it." Hirondelle's mastery of simple form, the deliberate compositions of space, plants, and art, are one artist's method of so arranging the world as to experience it most fully.

The Artist's Eye

Zen Minimalism: Inside the studio, Hirondelle creates still lifes with arrangements of found objects; pods, cones, feathers, leaves, old bird's nests. She continues this same deliberate arrangement of elements outside, using plants, space, and objects to create still lifes that form a new kind of garden room. She separates garden spaces as much by atmosphere, by the different sensation evoked as you enter, as by physical or visual barrier. At one side of a large open lawn, Hirondelle planted a Zen grove of small birches. She started out with five, but it didn't look right, so she planted a sixth. She then achieved the important uneven number of elements by adding a slender, three-foot ceramic vessel (made by Seattle artist Jim Kraft) whose color and crackled texture is as pale and rough as the bark of the birch saplings. There is nothing superfluous here, just the arrangement of tree trunks and pot, the contrast of their color and texture. The sun slanting over the hedge casts shadows from the trees that change the shape of the grove, accenting its feel of mystery and deep restfulness. Using only a few feet of space, six trees, and a pot, Hirondelle has created a meditation on how little is needed to make a garden that attracts and pleases in all seasons.

Blurring the Lines: Hirondelle uses simple techniques to blur the lines between indoors and out. Every horizontal surface is used as an opportunity for display: indoors she displays objects from nature, outdoors she uses man-made objects. The studio windowsills are lined with pods, cones, and leaves she has collected, placed as deliberately as if each were a precious piece of art. Outdoors a bench in the entry garden is treated as a similar surface for display, but here in the open air, indoor objects are lined up with the same regularity. The stone bench holds a series of vessels in graduated sizes; rainwater collects in the pots, reflecting the sky and providing a shimmering surface for floating blossoms. Hirondelle's artful pruning ("I prune everything all the time," she laughs) helps to bring the feel of the garden inside; trees are planted close to the studio and then limbed up so that the garden is viewed through leaves and branches. A profusely flowering *Clematis montana* is trained to droop low over the entry to the garden, linking house to studio, and garden to house. You push aside a curtain of flowers as you step into the inner courtyard from the street, and walk across pavers strewn with the pale clematis blossoms.

The Joys of Experimentation: "Sometimes I can see a form and just make it," says Hirondelle of the vessels that she models from clay. "Other times it is by trial and error." She is comfortable with experimentation in the garden, never drawing plans, but carving out beds to define space. Beds and borders keep evolving and growing larger. She received a birthday gift of a large ceramic vessel and needed somewhere to put it, so she dug a new bed in the center of the garden. Emphasizing that gardening is an intuitive thing, Hirondelle is free to enjoy the process because, as she says, "the garden is only for me." All is guided by her precision of planting, her strong aesthetic. "I love it when something wonderful turns out," says Hirondelle. "I can rarely take credit."

Nature's Palette: Though Hirondelle loves iris (one of the most architectural of flowers), and vines—more for their line than for their bloom—she never chooses plants for color but for shape and texture. A planting close to the studio is so lively with dynamic contrasts that it takes a close look to realize that it is nearly monochromatic. The bark of the pruned-up Japanese black pine looks even rougher in contrast to the smooth ribs of the hosta leaves at its base, its stark shape accented by their generously rounded forms. Green predominates throughout the garden—so much so that a clump of variegated iris with its yellow-striped blades looks nearly gaudy. The ceramic vessels placed among the plants keep to the same subtle scheme, their colors of brown, beige, and rust so organic they seem to have grown up from the soil just as much as the plants that surround them.

Form First: "Art is a form in the garden, more than a color or a texture," says Hirondelle. The simplicity of Hirondelle's plantings ensures that the clean, clear forms of the vessels will be the dominant artistic theme in the garden. Her pruning for architectural line and her choices of plants with bold and striking shapes, such as *Rodgersia* and iris, ensure that it is form that speaks most loudly throughout the garden. Color, texture, and flower are the usual language of the garden; here, they are heard as barely a whisper.

Far left: Wildlife artist Robert Bateman loves the peasant feel of this Italian olive oil jar and half-whiskey barrel holding a delicate Japanese maple.

Left: A detail of a Northwest Native American totem pole on the deck of Bateman's house.

3

Bestriding Juneau and Capri:
The Garden Ecosystems of Robert Bateman

The usual epithet for Robert Bateman is "wildlife artist," to which is appended some amplifying handle like "Canada's most renowned," "world's most successful," "wonderfully prolific," "multiple award–winning." And, yes, meticulously rendered, instantly recognizable wild animals do indeed gaze intently out from the foreground of Bateman's paintings—spotted owls and red foxes, spoonbill cranes and pronghorn antelopes, wolves and elephants, cheetahs and chaffinches. But if you spend enough time around Bateman's art, you realize that the animals are only part of the story. Equally important are the settings, the landscapes, the ecosystems in which the animals live. "He was one of the first to put his animal subjects into an environment," notes Rick Archbold, author of several books about Bateman and his work, including *Robert Bateman: An Artist in Nature*, "to create a painting that is an ecological whole."

Creating an ecological whole is an apt description of what Bateman has done with the garden that surrounds his house and studio on Saltspring Island in southern British Columbia. This is garden as habitat—an intimate, somewhat eccentric, carefully respectful interpretation of a coastal forest understory, with the canopy of firs and cedars, madrona and Garry oak left pretty much intact. Food, shelter, and water have been provided for resident and transient birds and other critters. Comfort, sun and shade, a variety of exposures, privacy, serenity, and fresh fruit, herbs, and flowers answer the needs of the human inhabitants. And for the artist, there is an ample supply of inspiration—in the sound of a stream purling over rocks in the shady garden around the north side of the house; in the spectacular views out to fjordlike Fulford Harbour; in the bright white sea-light that washes over the rocky bluff to which the flowers, vines, and fruit trees cling. What Bateman has done in his garden is to take what he loves best about the world and compress it into two intensively cultivated acres: art and nature, reflection and creation, wildlife and handicraft, shelter and exposure, adventure and meditation, food and flowers.

The approach to the Bateman garden is ravishing in itself, for Saltspring, the largest of the southern Gulf Islands and the closest to Victoria and the sprawl of lower Vancouver Island, is one of those ideal landscapes found only on affluent islands and in cherished, long-settled country places—a patchwork of tawny meadows and sheep pastures backing up into dense conifer forests, high ridges dropping down to deeply indented harbors, quiet lanes dotted with farmhouses and art galleries. At first glance, Bateman's garden looks like a slightly edited continuation of the surrounding landscape. Native Garry oaks and madronas tangle their boughs above masses of sword fern and rhododendron; a stream cascades and pools its way through the grounds, linking the cool shade garden at the house entrance with the sunny, dramatically exposed bluff on the "view" side; gates and trellises and little clusters of wooden outbuildings echo the vernacular style of the island's farms. In just a handful of years, Bateman has fashioned a garden that feels like an ancient, natural, and inevitable expression of the soil it springs from.

Below: Bateman crafted the banks of this pool out of artificial rocks and diverted the water from a seasonal stream.

Right: The many windows of Bateman's studio overlook the cool, damp, shady section of the garden he refers to as Alaska.

Which it isn't, by any stretch of the imagination. As it turns out, Bateman's garden, for all its naturalism and wildlife-friendliness, is even more staged and scripted than most. The rocks that give it backbone, the course of the stream that meanders through, the very profile of the outcrop that looms over the sea have all been painstakingly fabricated, inserted, moved, altered, played with, redirected, built up, or pared back. As Bateman confesses modestly, "God did the bluff, but all the rest is my attempt to make it look like it just happened. The garden is contrived to look uncontrived. The same principle applies in my garden and my art."

You see exactly what he means when you study one of his monumental canvases of polar bears clinging to an arctic ice floe or mountain goats grazing a Rocky Mountain meadow. The artifice, the brushstrokes, the personality and point of view of the creator have all been carefully disguised so that the image seems translated from wilderness to painting without human intervention. Unless you know where to look, you'd be hard pressed to find signs of Bateman either in his paintings or in his garden: he's adept at covering his tracks. This instinctive, unobtrusive reverence for the natural world has also inspired him to take a major role in international environmental activism, which is the other pillar of his life. It is important to Bateman as an artist, a committed environmentalist, and a member of a fragile island community to make a garden that harmonizes with its setting to the point of disappearing into it.

A handsome, trim, clear-featured, blue-eyed, fair-haired man who looks at least a decade younger than his sixty-nine years and acts like someone half that age, Bateman has an incredibly busy schedule—his travels, international exhibitions, and environmental activism keep him on the road two-thirds of the year—but he knows how to make the most of his time. In the midst of the worldly clamor of success—fame, fortune, major exhibitions including a one-man show at the Smithsonian Institution, commissions including one from the Canadian government to paint a wedding present for Prince Charles and the late Princess Diana, a slew of awards and honorary degrees, incessant demands on his time and checkbook—Bateman remains centered, outwardly serene, alive to the random, fleeting pleasures of the natural world.

To understand the character and "feel" of the garden, he explains, standing just inside the first and most elaborate of a series of African-motif gates, it's useful to consider the two radically different exposures his property enjoys: northeast in the front, southwest around the other side—the water view side. Bateman likes to think of the northeast exposure as the Alaska/Japan side and the southwest as the Mediterranean. He points to a thriving clump of Garry oaks over on the Mediterranean as an illustration of how radically different these two microclimates are: "Garry oaks don't grow in Vancouver. In fact, they're usually thought of as California trees. But they grow here on Saltspring Island, along with madrona trees, on well-drained southwest-facing slopes. These sunny southwest exposures are an endangered ecosystem in southwestern Canada because real estate developers are so fond of them. That's why it's so important to protect every Garry oak."

Bateman's Mediterranean is certainly a dazzling, bold, theatrical space with riotously colorful cliffside plantings reminiscent of the Amalfi coast—sweet peas, lavender, lilies, woolly thyme, peonies, heather, rosemary, chives, dill, raspberries, strawberries, *Caryopteris,* vine maples, dwarf apple and plum trees—all mixed up together in loose painterly borders and patches. Surrounding these quaint, informal beds are sweeping trellises of fragrant old climbing roses—'The Garland', much prized by Gertrude Jekyll, and 'Bloomfield Abundance'—and wisteria that frame views of the harbor and Mount Maxwell beyond. Decks set on several tiers, both freestanding and sprouting off the house, hold pots, arbor-shaded picnic tables, a hot tub, and large rectangular planters jammed with annuals

Left: The "mother of all bird feeders" attracts scores of varieties of winged guests. In the foreground, artificial rockwork Bateman fashioned out of molded concrete "cookies."

Right: Gates, trellises, courtyards, and leafy tunnels abound in Bateman's garden.

that act as flowering railings. The warm, sea-lit Mediterranean fairly vibrates with color, scent, and bees on a sunny summer day. But Bateman freely admits that this is really the realm of his wife Birgit, an artist who weaves and rug-hooks colorful abstract compositions. Much as he loves the view of the sea over the bluff and the way the wind has carved and twisted the exposed Douglas firs, Bateman's heart is in Alaska/Japan.

The plant palette of the Alaska side runs to ordinary shade-loving Northwest natives—sword ferns, deer ferns, mosses, rhododendrons—along with bits of unobtrusive exotics like sweet woodruff, ivy, bluebells, cotoneaster, vinca, lady's mantle. It's an understory garden designed to accent and complement the existing forest cover of madrona and cedar. For contrast with the many shades of green, Bateman has placed a red Japanese maple in a half barrel near a startling umber Italian olive oil jar set in an artful niche; in late spring clumps of *Ceanothus* unfurl a border of pure blue at the fenced frontier between Alaska and the Mediterranean; and in summer white and pale yellow flecks of Alpine strawberries catch the filtered sunlight. There's one more spot of color that shows when you get up close: the yellow cracked corn that spills from what Bateman calls "the mother of all bird feeders," a cross between a Balinese shrine and an avian soup kitchen, set on a rise amid ferns, Japanese holly, vinca, and Irish moss in the middle of Alaska so that Bateman can see it easily from his studio window.

Welcome and interesting as these blotches of color are, they are present more as relief than as main event. What's really going on in Alaska is a subtle and soothing evocation of a temperate forest—not a recreation of a hillside glade but the interpolation of sylvan vignettes and associations into the existing landscape: the flicker of shadow on glossy leaves, a ray of light haloing a pine bough, the trill of song sparrows or the

Left: Viewed from the shore, Bateman's garden rises in a series of tiers knit together by flowing and standing water.

Right: This sculptural collection of driftwood is actually a funky boathouse that a friend constructed for Bateman.

splash of water on stone. "The sound of flowing water is a bell ringing in your heart," remarks Bateman, gazing blissfully down at a little cascade he fashioned. "It gives a subliminal sense of joy." Bateman feels the same joy when the flowing water comes in the form of rain. "The garden is really at its best in winter," he muses. "It's lovely when it rains." And when it snows too, to judge by the moody, gauzy snow scene Bateman photographed after a recent freak snowstorm, all white humps slashed by black branches.

In a way, Bateman's Alaska epitomizes that ever-elusive horticultural grail: the Northwest garden style. No one has ever satisfactorily defined exactly what this style is, but you know it when you see it. And Bateman's shade garden is it: the dense tapestry of green and evergreen, the pitched rugged site, the presence of water, the exalted use of humble materials, the reverent integration of the native forest cover, the sense of benevolent mystery and mossy fecundity. Understatement prevails—no hot colors or loud noises permitted here. It's a garden that rewards long contemplation. If you back away to take in the big picture, you'll notice that a series of uprights—rocks tilting skyward, skinny leaning tree trunks, aspiring fern fronds—runs through Bateman's Alaska like a miniature mountain range, adding a strong vertical component. (Bateman confesses that the garden was originally oriented around horizontals, but when it dawned on him during a recent trip to Japan that vertical lines prevail in the traditional Japanese garden, he tore everything up and redid it.) Now approach one of the rocks and take a close look—what appears to be lichen is actually a painting of lichen done by Bateman. Details matter.

Again, there's a close parallel here with his art. As Canadian editor and writer Ramsay Derry notes in *The Art of Robert Bateman*, the clarity of detail and "wealth of information" in Bateman's paintings "make them so instantly understandable to a viewer that it requires an effort to look beyond the subject matter to appreciate the handling of space and depth, the subtle presentation of mood, and the powerful and recurring abstract shapes." In the garden, one way to appreciate Bateman's manipulation of space and mood and abstraction is to scrutinize the "bones"—the architectural elements that define the major areas and the relationship between plantings and house. "I love cloisters in Europe and little courtyards," says Bateman. "I like the sense of walking through tunnels and arbors." In his garden, he has translated this fondness

Left: Bateman has built a series of "pauses" into his garden, using pools, potted plants, and art works to capture the eye and focus the attention.

Right: Bateman's "Alaska" is a miniature coastal forest embraced and sheltered by his house.

for enclosure into a network of leafy tunnels and loose, informal courtyards, most of them built around little pools of water.

Bateman has always had a passion for travel—he took his first around-the-world trip by Land Rover in 1957 when he was twenty-seven—and the structures and objects in his garden are in a sense shrines to the places he loves best. The lozenge-and-diamond pattern repeated on gates and doorways comes from the entry to a chief's compound Bateman admired in Nigeria. Peak-roofed wooden lanterns scattered in the shady entry garden are Bateman's scaled-down version of lanterns he remarked at the great Shinto shrine of Ise, "one of the four or five most spiritual places in the world," in his opinion. The statue of a crane pausing by a piece of driftwood comes from Kyoto. The totem pole that graces the deck near his front door is, of course, Northwest Native American. Bateman half-jokingly refers to the garden's mélange of objects, references, and associations as "the universal peasant style," and indeed a lot seems to be going on at once in a two-acre plot, but it works.

Part of what holds the composition together is the sense of flow: both the flow of water from a stream that Bateman has diverted so that it spills through his garden in a series of gentle cascades alternating with small pools and, harmonizing with the running water, the flow of space that he has fashioned through angled paths, fixed and living screens, gates, steps, stepping stones, trellises, and "pauses"—unobtrusive platforms where one naturally lingers for a moment to gaze at a wooden owl mask, the glowing needles of a lone Japanese pine gracing a half barrel, a last spray of foxglove, or a sword fern frond floating in a dapple of sun. "The idea in my garden is to twinkle your way through and explore and be a little confused," Bateman remarks. "Modernism is not me."

This sense of "twinkling" your way in slight confusion through tunnels, cloisters, and levels carries over into the house, a wonderfully complex, multitiered, post-and-beam fabrication with a rambling kitchen as its heart (you can see both Alaska and the Mediterranean while you cook), a series of decks in strategic places, and an immense, airy, irregularly shaped studio with a greenhouse-like bank of windows perched on top. It's the kind of house where you never quite know what floor you're on or which door to open.

Back outside, as he strolls through a gate that separates Alaska from the Mediterranean, Bateman points to a patch of exposed bluff that has been carefully left untended: brown grass combed by the wind, bare elbows of rock, a few stunted shrubs. This is a stark, and actually quite beautiful, reminder of what the southwest exposure would look like without water or imported, cultivated plants—precisely how the property was when he acquired it.

Bateman loves to recount one rather grandiose scheme he hatched to soften the "bare-ass" look of the exposed western side of the house. After the original house was remodeled, the view from the living room was rather stark, and Bateman decided he needed a large tree right outside the window, both as a screen from curious boaters and as a weather-beaten focal point. He spotted the specimen he wanted in an island farm field—a mature, 35-foot tall, interestingly twisted Douglas fir—and went to considerable expense of time and money to move it. A kind of railway skid had to be constructed from his driveway, through Alaska and around to the west side of the house; he rented a flatbed truck and hired some strong backs to help with the digging and lifting. "It took a full day to transplant," he recalls. "They had to close town to traffic when we came through. Before we moved the tree, we marked the south and west compass points on the tree trunk so we would know which way to orient it—after all, trees have feelings. We said a few hopeful prayers when we set it in the ground and watered it in." The tree went into a ten-foot-deep recessed planter Bateman had constructed next to the house. (He later covered it with molded cement "rocks" to make it look like a natural cliff face and added sprays of kinnikinnick and Shasta daisies.) At first Bateman stabilized the fir by fastening the trunk to the house, but it has taken firm root and flourished and is now, in his opinion, the healthiest tree on the shore. Quite a production for one tree—but to Bateman it was worth it, and it makes a great story.

Bateman, who was born in Toronto and lived much of his life near that lake city, says that part of the reason he moved to the West Coast was to see the ocean every day—but when you tour his garden with him, you hear far more about the little stream he diverted than about the immense blue prospect that opens up at land's end. The image of freshwater pools perched above the salt sea has always tugged hard on his imagination—the counterpoint of scale, the sense of flow and return—and he has arranged the garden to make the most of this image. Follow the stream and you'll find the secret cords that bind the garden design together. Slipping into the eastern edge of Bateman's property through a dense stand of conifers, the stream relaxes near the house into a dark mossy pool at the far reaches of Alaska, then passes under the house to emerge through a wooden pipe in the light green shade of a grape arbor: Juneau to Capri in the twinkling of an eye.

Left: Bateman's "Mediterranean" is drenched in bright light reflected off the water of fjordlike Fulford Harbour.

Right: Robert Bateman at work in his airy, upstairs studio.

The Artist's Eye

Stonework to Fool the Eye: Bateman always wondered how zoos and natural history museums got their fake cliffs to look so real. Then he learned the secret from the display designers at the Royal British Columbia Museum in Victoria: they take molds of real cliff faces. Bateman's garden is full of these natural-looking artificial cliffs and rocks, which he jokingly refers to as "cookies"; practically the entire stream flows through a cookie course that he fashioned himself. Here's his recipe. Find a cliff side in nature that you really like and paint latex casting compound (available at art supply stores) on it, then put cheesecloth over the latex. Repeat until you have five layers, then let the mold dry and peel it off the rock. Now, to make the cookie, press a layer of concrete into the mold and reinforce it with embedded chicken wire, leaving a two-inch border of chicken wire on all sides. Repeat until you have a batch of cookies. To build a cliff, waterfall, or pool, wire together as many cookies as you need, mortar over the joints, and hide the seams with stones. Pack soil into holes and gaps and plant with ferns, lady's mantle, and so on—and voilà! Naturalistic artificial stonework. As a final touch, Bateman sometimes paints bits of lichen on the finished surface, or paints the entire rock face to make it blend in with its surroundings. He also smears yogurt on some cookies to encourage moss and lichens to colonize them.

Taking Advantage of Microclimates: Bateman's designations "Alaska" and "Mediterranean" are rather fanciful, but they reflect a keen appreciation of his property's microclimates. In fact, these two exposures present radically different growing conditions just a few feet apart. Rather than try to push the envelope or fight the givens, Bateman has incorporated existing landscape and climate conditions into his garden design and made the best of them. Running water accentuates the cool elfin feel of the Alaska woodland, while pools dotted with lily pads reflect the sky on the exposed Mediterranean side. Bateman has neither suppressed nor clear-cut the lush coastal forest on the north side, but instead he uses it as the inspiration for his understory garden. The Alaska shade garden "feels" like a fine-tuning of nature: it harmonizes with what has always been there and provides shelter and food for woodland animals.

Sparing Use of Color: In a shade garden, such as Bateman's Alaska, the rare splash of color really stands out against the dark green backdrop. A tub of ordinary New Guinea impatiens becomes an eye-catching centerpiece because there are no competing reds or oranges around it all summer long. Similarly, the red Japanese maple growing in a half whiskey barrel takes on a rich, spotlit glow, especially in autumn, against the surrounding greens of ferns, ivies, and mosses.

Ingenious Deer Fences: Deer are a problem on Saltspring Island, as in many rural areas, and Bateman came up with an ingenious and appealing way of keeping them out of his garden. "Everyone told me I'd need a seven- to nine-foot fence to keep out deer," he says, "but I didn't want the garden to feel like a prison camp. Well, I know a bit about deer psychology and I used that in designing my deer fence." Bateman figured that deer would be afraid of entangling their legs in a wide fence, so he constructed a kind of trellis with upright posts that rise four feet high, topped by horizontal crosspieces at right angles that extend out two feet on the outside and one foot on the inside. The effect is a series of slightly rickety looking T's with the vertical members set two feet apart. Spaces can be filled in with four-inch wire mesh or decorative slats. The fence is low enough to be unobtrusive, wide enough to ward off deer (not a single one has ever crossed into the garden), and the ideal support for all sorts of wonderful vines and creepers such as wisteria and honeysuckle.

Architectural Elements: "There is a lot of architecture in the garden," notes Bateman, pointing to the fences, gates, screens, lanterns, the towering bird feeder, and the "tunnels" and "cloisters" he has created with trellises covered with climbing and rambling plants like wisteria and roses. Repeating patterns on the gates set up a kind of rhythm that echoes between different parts of the garden. Though he has drawn on the styles of many different countries in these structures, he avoids a feeling of busyness or hodgepodge by relating the roofline, profile, and decorative elements of gates, screens, and so forth to the house and the terrain of the property.

Far left: Sculptor Les Bugajski always carves the eyes of his stone men first, so he can meet who it is he's working on.

Left: The white-flowered annual *Bacopa* forms the tail of a white dove Bugajski painted into a recess on his toolshed.

A Storyteller at Heart:
The Garden of Les Bugajski

Every morning, very early, Les Bugajski walks down the back steps of his house and through his long, narrow garden to his workshop. Here he carves stone and distresses and shapes wood to make forms that are at once useful, decorative, and downright haunting. His creations, both for his own garden and for clients throughout the Northwest, include custom wooden benches and railings, carved faces in stone and wood, and entire garden plans. His own garden is a living, green, theatrical workshop,

Below: Les Bugajski standing amid a collection of dwarf conifers in his meticulously maintained garden.

Right: Each carved face in the garden reflects the inherent and unique characteristics of the piece of wood or stone from which Bugajski fashions his creations.

where he plays with ideas and materials, creating stories out of stone and wood, flower and foliage. Not stories in words, but more fragile, evanescent stories, made up of images and intimations. Who is that old man whose beard is caught in the curve of an aged log? What gnarled face holds up the rockwork of the pond, and what child once skipped down these lawns to pause at the bench beneath the curved arbor? This is the garden of a woodworker and stone carver by trade, a storyteller at heart.

For any gardener a simple morning walk-through usually takes far more time than intended. There are always faded blossoms to pluck, slugs to destroy, weeds to pull. The morning walk for Bugajski is his delight, his chance to tidy his near-immaculate garden, to feed the frogs and fish in the pond, to commune with the faces of the old men who haunt the garden. But the many trellises, smoothly shaped benches, and stone faces in the garden are evidence that Bugajski has, often enough, reached his studio.

Artists shape their gardens, but so, too, do gardens shape artists; and the siren call of Bugajski's own garden keeps him at home nearly every day of the year. His world is here, in his garden and studio, sited on a level, open street in a neighborhood of modest homes in Vancouver, Washington. A dark-blond ponytail streams over one shoulder of his plaid shirt, his blue eyes crinkle up when he smiles; this lean and lively man leads tours of his garden for dozens of garden enthusiasts every weekend all summer. Bugajski's modesty and friendly grin are deceptive, for this is a complex man of many experiences, an immigrant from Poland at the age of ten, a teller of tales, a master illusionist who uses the garden as a living backdrop to enhance his work in wood and in stone. It would be hard to find a man more enamored of garden-making, more in love with his art and his craft—yet Bugajski's pleasure in his garden must barely match that of his visitors once they pass through the fence into the enchanted back garden.

When Bugajski and his wife, Cindy, bought their house four years ago, their half-acre back garden was an old horse pasture, a blank canvas except for a couple of overgrown rhododendrons, a big maple tree, and two huge Doug firs. The amount of work it took to create such lushness of planting and detail of structure in just a few years is daunting, but Bugajski is full of energy. "I always

have a project going," he says. He has brought in more than 3,200 plants, creating a mix of foliage and flowers that, in the benign climate of southern Washington State, keeps the garden going for nine months of the year.

Bugajski is that rare hybrid, an artist possessed of a deep need for orderliness, and his beautiful garden reflects this paradox: it is at once perfectly tidy yet abundantly planted, and better yet, full of enchanting and startling surprises. Scrupulous attention to detail is apparent everywhere you turn. The healthy exuberance and appeal of plantings so consummately groomed and trimmed and tidied might reform the messiest of gardeners. One of the many cleverness of this garden is that Bugajski's tidy nature hasn't detracted from the essence of the plants. All this luxuriance enhances his artwork, at once framing and partially obscuring it.

The three old trees lend scale and provide shade in the large rectangle of the back garden. But it takes more than old trees to create the feeling of age, even venerability, that graces this spot. Bugajski has worked an artist's magic to give this flat, fenced space in a Vancouver neighborhood the feel of an established European garden. It could be the garden of a Swiss chalet, or small estate alongside an Austrian lake, cared for by a single family for generations. "When I walk away from a landscape, it looks a hundred years old," explains Bugajski. It is his use of stone, carefully chosen, placed, or carved, and the techniques he uses to distress wood that trick the eye, engage the heart and bring the visitor into the many stories Bugajski is telling here.

Bugajski's carvings of faces are the most powerful and haunting images in the garden. Sinuously slender forms with lined faces and bristly beards peer out of hollowed logs; stones in the wall that supports the round, raised fishpond have eyes, nose, mouth, and whiskers. Like snowflakes or the stars in the sky, each face is unique and individual, gazing upon the garden from where it has been nestled into the foliage. The curved forms of whole logs and uncarved stones softened with moss are placed just as carefully as painstakingly crafted works of art. These natural forms, untouched by human

Below: Bugajski's trompe l'oeil paintings add to the narrative quality of the garden.

Right: A grassy pathway lined with daylilies curves beneath a wisteria bedecked arbor as it leads to one of Bugajski's distressed wood benches.

hands except in gathering them from the woods and mountains, add to the guilelessness of the faces set among them. Perhaps they just grew here . . .

"I use lots of faces in the garden so that I'm never alone," says Bugajski. Why is it always the faces of old men that he carves? He says that he has long been intrigued by the character found in the wrinkled faces of old men. He looks closely at the stone as he works, and just sees what comes out as he carves. Each face reflects the unique and individual character of the stone it is fashioned from. "I always carve the eyes first," explains Bugajski, "and then I meet who it is I'm working on."

Statuary has traditionally been used to express the essential spirit of the garden. The grand garden sculptures of the Romans served as trophies of travels and conquests. The Victorians, with their affinity for pomp, used the nymph and the nude to emphasize tradition and formality. Bugajski's stone faces are in the tradition of Renaissance garden statuary, rich with complicated allegory. This tradition of storytelling in the garden was eclipsed when the garden itself became expressive in the eighteenth-century English landscape style; but up until then, anyone with the right education could read a garden like a book. Bugajski's carvings hold this promise of a story, of history contained in a face; but in their tactile, organic nature they seem to have grown up out of the ground itself. And despite their seemingly random positions, peeking out from beneath a leaf or the curve of a tree, the faces are cunningly placed to lead you deeper into the garden as surely as signposts along a hidden trail.

Coaxing a shape from a piece of stone calls for patient and exacting work. The deliberate, unhurried pace of sculpting in stone seems better suited to the nineteenth century than to the speeded-up dawn of the twenty-first. Stonework connects the artist as well as the viewer to the earth, to long, slow time both in the working of the stone and in the fact that these faces could last a thousand years—an intriguing contrast to the ephemeral plants that surround them. These are tactile works of art and as one gazes at them the fingers are drawn irresistibly to stroke the beards of the old men, to touch the lips or to smooth the brows. There is breath and life itself in the stones of the craggy faces. Sitting on the edge of the pond, one expects to feel a rustle at the ankle, a puff of air from the old man's mouth. What is most striking about Bugajski's sculpture is its narrative quality: these faces set

Left: Purple-flowering potted annuals spark a shady planting of yellow-splashed *Aucuba japonica* 'Gold Dust', *Hosta* 'Blue Moon', and the purple-veined *Heuchera micrantha* 'Pewter Moon'.

Right: The face of an old man peeks out from its base of the raised fish pond.

in the lush profusion of his back garden tell stories of the old country, of times past, of things that might have been.

Swaths of open lawn and curved pathways give passage through the garden, beneath trees and arbors, alongside raised planting beds, through shade and into sunlight. As Bugajski walks through the garden, gesturing and explaining with the inflections of a man born to a different language, the garden unfolds its treasures one by one, just as the pages of a book are turned. Here, you are invited to pause at a shady bench beneath a twiggy arbor and drink in the scent of pink Oriental lilies. A little farther along, a smoothly carved bench tempts you to rest and caress its burnished wood. The sound of water bubbling over stones and the flash of goldfish lure you to pause at the raised pond, its little wall just the right height for sitting, its edging stones flat and clean. Ferns, azaleas, sweet woodruff, and the tricolored leaves of *Houttuynia cordata* 'Chameleon' cascade over the rocks, while a stone man you've no doubt heard of in Norse legends spits a cascade of water over plants into the pond. At the back of the garden alongside Bugajski's studio is a cobbled patio furnished with picnic table, benches, and purple umbrella, surrounded by a colorful medley of variegated dogwood, dwarf conifers, petunias, and verbena. A graceful nude female torso emerges from a clump of tall sedums to preside over this farthest corner of the garden.

The plants in Bugajski's garden set the stage for his art. Carved and painted railings, smooth curves of natural wood in arbors and benches, trompe l'oeil paintings on a fence, all tell the tales of gardens past, landscapes of the memory. And yet utility is never sacrificed to fancy. Take the garden shed. It is the most charming of little houses set into a corner of the larger garden, with its own weathered picket fence and mossy stone pathway leading to the peeling front door flanked with

Left: Carved posts and niches embellished with plants and paintings lend a feel of mystery and stories untold.

Right: An example of Bugajski's planting style of mixing annuals, perennials, shrubs, and trees all together.

window boxes. The shed evokes mystery, prompts a story. Who might live there? What child left the cherished Speedaway sled hanging on the back wall? Did a horse from the old pasture throw the shoe that's hung, no doubt for luck, on the old barn-wood siding? A nook hollowed out of the shed's side holds an overflowing pot of *Bacopa* and the blurry carving of a white bird in flight; it might serve as an altar, or as a window into another reality. The shed's tiny fenced front garden is filled with bright cottagey flowers, while in the back garden a picket fence runs up alongside a larger, solid fence that offers painted panoramas of distant pastures, trees, mountains, and sky. In reality, the intriguing little garden house is simply a handy toolshed, and the tall fence is primarily a privacy shield from the neighbor's house next door. Bugajski has turned a utilitarian structure into the garden shed of a hundred stories, decorated and designed to stir not only nostalgia but also the imagination and the emotions.

What started out as a flat and featureless yard now compels admiration not only for its abundance of healthy, well-orchestrated plantings but for its feel of age and venerability, miraculously achieved in only four years. Bugajski has created a stage set of a garden, an outdoor magical mystery tour. Although plants are the fiber, texture, and color of the garden, his imaginative carvings, paintings and sleight-of-hand are its wonder, its distinction, and its soul.

Left: Though Bugajski started his garden only four years ago, it feels much more established and mature because of the vast number of plants (some 3,200 in all).

Right: The stone faces used throughout the garden hold the promise of a story, of history in the expression of eyes and mouth.

The Artist's Eye

Function First: Bugajski's ingeniousness lies in his ability to combine artistry with utility, resulting in garden art that is integral to the mood and form of the garden, not mere decoration. The carvings always relate to the structure of the garden. The water that fills the garden with music pours out between the mossy lips of a stone man's face; other faces peer out from smoothly shaped logs that support arbors and add vertical punctuation; still others support the raised pond.

Recycled and Distressed Materials: Bugajski uses salvaged materials throughout his garden. He has ferreted out worn barn wood, battered doors, aged mirrors and window frames. He took an inexpensive metal shed and framed it out, covering it with old barn wood, and then added paned mirrors for windows (if he had used real glass in the windows, the rakes, shovels, and hoses resting inside would show). When he cut down some old and leggy rhododendrons, he preserved the twisted trunks to reuse in pergolas that arch over pathways. When he is unable to find old materials, he distresses new wood, sanding, staining, and splintering it, to add age and personality, creating layers of history in each fence, bench, or arbor.

Mixing It Up: Bugajski says his wife is the one who reads the gardening books. He himself plants fearlessly, heedless of rules or conventions, mixing all kinds of plants together: needled conifers consort with small deciduous trees, lilies bloom above the most common and the most unusual of groundcovers. He is not a plant snob; rather, he strives to grow each plant as well as he can so that it achieves its full potential. He is constantly learning. "We try to use everything, to learn what it does, and how it grows here." He is not afraid to mix traditions or genres either; his stone faces evoke Europe, while in a shady corner, amid pebbles and ornamental grasses, water bubbles out of the top of a mossy dark stone Buddha's head that he has carved.

Hidden Treasure: How Bugajski uses art in the garden is as important as what he uses. Each face and carving is part of the story, sometimes a footnote, often a starting place for the imagination. Each element is placed beneath and amidst plants to surprise and delight, instead of to confront or overwhelm. None of the pieces in the garden says "Look at me" the way a sculpture often does when it's mounted on a pedestal or placed as a focal point in the center of a lawn. Instead, each element is strategically placed to take advantage of a bit of shade, to bring intrigue to a dark corner, to lead the eye to the next bend in the path and beyond, so that the garden as a whole feels like a treasure hunt, with plenty of bounty to be enjoyed again and again.

Far left: A preening peacock shares outdoor gallery space with the monumental metalwork of Oregon sculptor Lee Kelly.

Left: Kelly fabricates metal into shapes so tactile that they invite comparisons to tree bark and beach stones.

Contemplating the Monumental:
The Sculpture Garden of Lee Kelly

The Oregon countryside south of Portland is plushly green and pleated into soft rolls, punctuated with majestic evergreen trees bred of the rich soil and drizzly climate. Narrow country roads wind through hillsides speckled white and brown with grazing sheep. A peacock, proudly dragging his jeweled plumage across the gravel of the driveway leading to Lee Kelly's garden, seems as out of place here as the huge sculpture he huffily flies up to perch on. The puff of his royal blue chest, the jaunty angle of his tail, clearly indicate the bird's belief that the rusted metal piece rests in this bucolic setting solely to serve as his pedestal. This notion is no more incongruous than finding so many of Kelly's industrial-scale pieces sitting here beneath the trees, alongside the country road; no more surprising than that the old barn at the end of the rutted driveway houses a working foundry, producing mammoth sculptures destined for cities around the country.

One of the Northwest's most respected and prolific sculptors, Kelly has lived on this five-acre preserve for nearly forty years. A lean and rangy man in his late 60s, wearing old Levis and a shirt with rolled-up sleeves, Kelly exudes a contemplative calm as he walks through the forest he has planted, pausing by the metal constructions he has fabricated. His exuberant eyebrows, thick and snow-white, are his most animated feature; they jump about in contrast to his wide, slow grin and broad gestures as he tells of the varied international influences that have shaped his aesthetic for both his work and his garden. Perhaps only a man so long anchored in the verdancy of Oregon could think of placing such machine-age work amid the trees, would have the facility to shape metal into forms so tactile that they invite comparisons to beach stones and tree bark.

Kelly was born in McCall, Idaho, but came to Oregon to attend high school and college and stayed on to teach college art, winning an Oregon Governor's Award for the Arts and an Oregon Masters Fellowship in Sculpture. Lest any of this sound provincial, Kelly travels to far corners of the earth "to feed my art habit. I don't go many different places, but I tend to go back over and over again to the same places." He has climbed mountains in Nepal, traveled to Mexico to study the Mayan culture, and learned traditional bronze-casting methods from artists in Katmandu. One of his sculptures is displayed in Japan, and the memory of the fireplace he welded for a bar in Katmandu brings a grin to his face.

Right: Lee Kelly in front of one of his new metal pieces.

Far right: Trees and fences are sometimes placed to stop the eye, and in other spots positioned to lead a visitor toward a piece of sculpture.

Henry Moore, Britain's best known twentieth-century sculptor, liked to display his work outdoors on a stretch of open lawn or field. "Sculpture gains by finding a setting that suits its mood, and when that happens, there is a gain for both sculpture and setting," Moore said of his sculpture garden, which still exists today in the

British countryside. Lee Kelly's monolithic pieces seem equally at home beneath the tall trees and woodland plantings that have grown up to give them context and scale. The starkness of their shapes, their girth and solidity might appear overwhelming or even disturbing if they rose out of an open field; but when they are set among the gentle, sheep-dotted hills and tall, leafy trees, the metal is softened and the size subdued, as well as invested with the meaning of the surroundings. For Kelly's garden has grown to become not only workplace and gallery but family compound and family memorial.

"The artwork is the human presence in the garden, the spirit of the place," explains Kelly. He sees the garden as a meeting place between the man-made environment and the natural one; his job has been to create a natural setting that can come halfway to meet his sculpture. Kelly has shaped his corner of the countryside into an exercise in yin and yang, of rough and finished, raw and smooth. The abstraction of the welded metal pieces plays off organic forms: tree, shrub, passing deer. Their sheer metal bulk emphasizes the fragility of nature. The hunkered-down, heavy permanence of the sculptural forms contrasts with the ephemeral nature of the garden that surrounds them. The silent, timeless presence of the huge pieces is nearly overwhelming, with each casting a metaphoric shadow far surpassing its actual size. Despite their being fabricated of metal, the sculptures exude a sense of the archaic and elemental, as if each work had sprung from footfalls printed on the earth by the largest dinosaurs. Surely these pieces are as old, as integral to the landscape, as the cedars and Douglas firs that tower above them. Every corner turned brings a glimpse of towering rusted metal or shiny sheets of stainless steel shaped into monolithic pieces that glow quietly in the shade of the trees, their luminosity reflecting even the feeblest shaft of sunlight that penetrates the forest. This sense of permanence is deceptive. Kelly explains that few of the pieces are permanently sited. "Sometimes I even sell one!" he laughs, almost as if reminding himself that this acreage is not only home, foundry, and sculpture garden but also gallery.

The garden is so naturalistic that one might easily assume that it somehow grew up to embrace, enclose, and enhance the sculptures, to gild the metal pieces with colorful leaves in autumn and lighten them with flowers in spring. The truth is that when Kelly and his wife, Bonnie Bronson, bought five acres of old dairy farm in the 1960s and moved south from Portland, they thinned out the existing scrub (all the firewood used on the property is still cut here) and then planted more than 2,000 trees, to give privacy and lend scale to the work Kelly was creating. They planted Doug firs, vine maples, birches, sequoias. ("I wish I'd been more careful," sighs Kelly—a familiar gardeners' lament decades down the road. "It was a great day when the trees grew tall enough to thin out and look between.") After the trees were in place, they brought in understory ferns and vinca to try to outcompete the blackberries, with which Kelly still struggles. Over the years, though, the birds and the volunteer plants have created an entirely different understory. "I tried hostas for awhile—but they didn't work," says Kelly. Viburnums, gangly shrubs with leathery leaves, have proved much more satisfactory and deer resistant, and are planted throughout the garden to lend a mid-story of shrubbery between groundcovers and tree canopy.

Bronson and Kelly's master plan emphasized visual corridors and a path system that has served the property well for decades. Kelly says, "The purpose was to place the work, and lead visitors to it—I planned it around what I wanted visitors to see." Large plants were put in close to the buildings, to "bury" house, cabins, and barn in the landscape, and grouped to create outdoor rooms and groves to emphasize certain pieces and groupings of sculpture. The visual corridors direct the eye not only to these groupings but beyond the boundaries of the property to the green and folded pastures of Kelly's neighbors. Kelly has skillfully used the Japanese concept of borrowed scenery (he refers to the technique as "blurring the boundaries") to emphasize the landscape's contours and to screen out other houses. Trees and fences are positioned to stop the eye in some spots, and in others to lead the eye beyond property lines to more distant vistas.

Left: The big old barn serves as both a backdrop for trees and sculpture, and as the fabrication studio.

Right: Kelly refers to his pieces as "alternative architecture" for their suggestion of doorways and windows.

The idea of garden rooms is not a new one. Fine examples exist today at Filoli in California and at Vita Sackville-West's Sissinghurst in England. At first the Kelly garden appears to be a large and simple woodland, surrounding a barn, a house, and several cabins. Its division into spaces or rooms subtly unfolds, as a carpet unrolls beneath the feet, as you are skillfully, seamlessly led into various parts of the garden that are divided by how each feels, by sun or shade, rather than by hedges or walls. Kelly refers to his sculptural pieces as "alternative architecture" for their suggestions of doorways, arches, and windows; thus the garden is divided into outdoor rooms as much by the sculptures themselves as by the plantings and the little wattle fences used as dividers.

As Kelly studied the art of different cultures, he also studied the history of their gardens, often finding the two inextricably entwined. He is a big fan of Moghul gardens, entranced by the idea that their architects were the emperors themselves. He loves the forms, the intricate spirals and mandala-like shapes, of Persian gardens. In India, he was impressed with how water was used for cooling, with marble waterways winding through gardens and into the center of buildings. "A garden is a meeting place between the everyday and the contemplative world," explains Kelly, sitting on his deck watching a deer graze alongside a flat rectangular metal pond that echoes the water gardens of India, its clouds, sky, and trees mirrored in its still surface. The sculptures that imbue the garden with spirit, which look so at home here beneath the cloudy Oregon skies, reflect Kelly's visual experience of Yucatan ruins, Nepalese temples, and Indian watercourses.

Kelly maintains a drawing studio in Portland, but creates and displays his large pieces here in the garden. The challenge in creating a setting for such sculpture

Left: The water gardens Kelly admired on his travels to India inspired this metal reflective pond, set into a bed of *Vinca minor*.

Right: "I wanted this piece to show energy and a positive outlook," says Kelly of his end-of-the-millennium memory sculpture, sited in a sunny meadow overlooked by grazing sheep.

is the scale in which Kelly works. Some of his pieces are immense, to thirty feet and higher (thus the need to plant sequoias), and the work is physically demanding (he uses cranes to move the metal parts about). One of Kelly's sculptures, *Bellgate*, stands outside Bellevue Square Mall, east of Seattle; kids and adults alike enjoy turning a crank at the bottom that moves curiously shaped, brightly

painted metal pieces as large as cars that sit atop the huge stainless-steel arches. Kelly also crafts residential-scale pieces, such as the round pool, filled with a curling spiral shape, that sits at a junction of two paths in the public garden outside of Portland known as Elk Rock, the Garden of the Bishop's Close.

The huge barn that Kelly has turned into his fabrication studio has old wooden siding and a metal roof. The living quarters he and his wife used to occupy are in the barn above the fabrication shop. Here warmth and intimacy are captured inside a rough exterior: hot orange walls ("I've never seen an orange I didn't like," says Kelly), plentiful bookshelves, brilliantly patterned and colored rugs, a metal wood-burning stove crafted by Kelly, and a deck that hangs out over the garden, positioned to be within earshot of the creek running through the property. Since Bonnie's death in 1990 in a climbing accident on Mount Adams, Kelly has lived in a small cabin in another corner of the property, one of his stainless-steel pieces right outside the kitchen window to provide visual relief from the task of washing dishes. Kelly's daughter and her family live in the property's original house; his son-in-law, a composer, has his music studio in a cabin marked by an arched sculpture with a flashing blue neon thunderbolt, softened by a climbing hydrangea. The arch of the sculpture is wired for sound; classical music pours out into the garden, joined by the ever-present background music of birds, neighboring horses and sheep, and the occasional wail of a peacock.

Kelly uses his garden not only as an outdoor gallery but also as a place to honor the memory of those he has loved, and these become monuments, part of the meaning of the garden. Bonnie, a gifted sculptor and collage artist, was influential in the birth of the garden, especially in the master planning and creation of the colorful, flowery meadow garden. Kelly scattered her ashes here, mixed with soil and wildflower seed. He created *The Bonnie Bronson Quartet* in her memory, a trio of steel towers suggesting rock climbing, engraved with names of places they had visited together, with the fourth element being a low altar in the middle. In another area of the garden is a memorial for their son Jason, who died of leukemia in 1978. His ashes are buried here, marked by a golden locust and aspens surrounding a temple built of rusted steel and accented with bright purple auto paint.

At one side of the property, alongside the road, Bronson and Kelly cleared a big, sunny meadow, which stirs Kelly's memories of Idaho ranches and gave space for Bonnie to grow vegetables, cut flowers, and herbs. This garden has been neglected since her death, but the archway to the garden still blooms with pink roses in summer. The meadow holds the memory piece that Kelly created for the end of the millennium. (Every ten years he has made a special memory piece as a way of loosely summing up the previous decade.) The structure exerts its own force field, drawing you to it like a kid to a jungle gym. You want not only to touch it but to climb up and explore its surfaces. How can so much mystery and humor be held within the geometry of rusted metal? "So much of what I do is emotionally heavy," says Kelly, "I wanted this piece to show energy and a positive outlook at the end of the decade." Set in a meadow along with sheep, peacocks, and metal fences, Kelly's construction stands as a hopeful vision of the future, his ideal of the collaboration between man and nature.

Left: Kelly has been strongly influenced by the organic forms of spiral and mandala found in Persian culture and gardens.

Right: "The artwork is the human presence in the garden, the spirit of the place," explains Kelly.

The Artist's Eye

Edited Elements: Edward Lutyens, the Edwardian architect and Gertrude Jekyll collaborator, said: "Every garden should have a backbone, a central idea beautifully phrased. Every wall, path, stone, and flower should have its relationship to the central idea." Kelly's sculpture garden might best be defined by what it is not; there are no flower borders, no ornamentation, no patio furniture (and no patios), no wide range of plants, no drip system, no mowed or edged lawns. The central idea here, to house and show off Kelly's sculptures because none of the Portland galleries were large enough to display them, has guided development of the garden for nearly four decades. Kelly and Bronson's master plan called for a mass planting of trees to form a canopy, groundcovers to keep out the weeds, and the creation of sight lines and pathways to direct the feet and the eye to the artworks. Over the years the garden has taken on a life of its own, become a majesty of metal, bark, vistas, sunlight, mood, and shadow that is so satisfying precisely because of its original purpose.

Cultural Borrowing: Despite the fact that Kelly works in geometric metal forms, he has been strongly influenced by the more organic forms of the spiral and the mandala, found in Persian gardens and culture. These have inspired him to work on a smaller scale and to create metal slabs ornamented with the spiral form, which are placed about on the forest floor of his Oregon sculpture garden. The use of water throughout gardens in India inspired Kelly's flat metal reflecting pond, set amid the groundcovers.

Playing with Scale: How to bring five acres, dotted with metal monolithic sculptures, down to human scale? Kelly began by planting hundreds of large trees that would in time create a canopy to give perspective and shelter to both the buildings and the sculpture. He blended the huge old barn into the acreage by surrounding it with Douglas fir, cedar, and sequoia trees that would grow up to partially obscure its steep metal roof and make it part of the garden itself, a backdrop to the sculpture. When the trees matured, Kelly began to thin them out to create visual corridors that lead the eye to his pieces, to special plants, to groupings of trees and sculptures.

Infusions of Color: Color could easily be lost amid the plentiful green and brown of the Kelly sculpture garden—tree bark, needles, and leaves predominate, along with the stainless steel or rusted metal of the sculptures. So, when Kelly does use color, it is eye-catching. You won't find pastels or washy colors here—they would just disappear. Kelly uses auto paint for its strong colors and durability. He applies his favorite colors, orange and blue, along with splashes of yellow, red, and purple. A stainless-steel grid is backed by a huge, flat sheet of Chinese red; the underside of a metal curve is painted a glowing purple.

A Celebration of Texture: The entire garden is a study of contrasts, the yin and yang of textural juxtapositions. The roughness of tree bark against the smooth shine of stainless steel, rusted metal softened by the fluff of new green leaves; the droop of weeping birches backing the erect thrust of a shiny, skyward-reaching column, the ephemera of autumn leaves tracing a pattern against the permanent bulk of chunky metal. Such diversity of texture is a surprise set amidst what is essentially a re-creation of a Northwest forest.

Directing the Eye and the Feet: Your journey through the Kelly sculpture garden, despite its feeling of surprise and discovery, is carefully orchestrated. You move as smoothly, as organically, from room to room as if a stream were ebbing and flowing, eddying about you, leading you onward. It is no accident that some of the pieces seem to nearly leap out at you while others are bracketed between trees, to be seen from a distance, as part of the landscape. Views of rolling pastures are "borrowed," neighboring houses are screened, and the edges of the property are effectively blurred with plantings and fences. The various outdoor rooms of the garden are divided as much by the feeling they evoke as by the sculptures and plants that divide them. Some areas are quietly contemplative, with smooth, rectilinear ponds reflecting sky and clouds; others are lively with nearly Klee-like pieces dangling bits of metal that wave about in the wind. These garden rooms are not just visual but are rich with emotional content and humor.

Far left: The bowling ball pyramid at the entrance to Nitzke Marquis's garden invites visitors to drop all their preconceptions about gardens, art, and garden art.

Left: An impromptu collage on the wall of a barn turned glass studio

Boxed Abundance:
The Garden Collages of Johanna Nitzke Marquis

Collage-construction artist Johanna Nitzke Marquis makes her art in boxes—indeed, the box itself is part of the art—so it was only natural when it came to garden-making that she would choose the box as her guiding design motif. Hers is an eccentric variation on the traditional walled or cloistered garden: protected and sheltered, fenced and gated and elaborately edged, intersected by paths, Nitzke Marquis's pleasingly geometric arrangement of garden boxes resides at the center of a mostly wooded ten-acre property on an island in Puget Sound. To get to the garden itself, to attain the tender heart inside, you must first pass through a series of rough outer layers—scruffy driveway, clumps of outbuildings, patches of meadow and lawn, cedar pickets, arbor-clad gate. This is garden as artichoke, as jewel lodged in the gem-box's innermost plush. The exact same process of moving through layers and levels of space happens in her "collage constructions"—the multimedia, three-dimensional, elegantly boxed and framed assemblages she creates in an enchanted hunter's hut doubling as a studio that peeks through climbing roses just outside the garden gate.

Nitzke Marquis is a collector—of old tools and buttons, seeds and twine and flea market figurines, dice and medicine bottles and picture frames, postcards and odd sayings—and she uses her art to display her collections to advantage, to conjure up fresh insights from striking juxtapositions, and to exult in the forms and colors and tantalizing promises of the natural and unnatural worlds. Nitzke Marquis is also a painter, and most of her constructions encase, radiate out from, swirl around, or recede into one of her paintings, usually a landscape with muted colors and sad washy-blue skies. Think Joseph Cornell collaborating with Gertrude Jekyll while Max Ernst and Georgia O'Keeffe peer over their shoulders and you'll have some sense of the lush, surreal aura of Nitzke Marquis's art.

Her garden is similarly stitched together out of serendipitous strokes, lucky finds, surprise volunteer plants, evocative mottoes, and weird intuitive pairings, all of it packed into and spilling out of a series of ingeniously constructed and artfully arranged boxes. In a sense, the garden is the art writ large. If you want to appreciate what she is doing in her collage constructions, ponder the tension between the rectilinear frames and wandering tendrils of form in the garden, let your eye drift from upright sprays of columbine to swooping wands of roses, read the inscriptions she has nailed to fence post and garden gate. Then return to the studio and consider the mass of cloth flowers, the beaded shoe, and the fancy buttons spilling out of a painting of a lonely country road, and the motto stamped

Left: Just as Nitzke Marquis incorporates frames into the overall design of her collage constructions, so she embellishes fences and weaves them into her garden compositions.

Right: Sprays of lupine, spires of 'Nora Balow' columbine, and sweet woodruff soften the straight lines of fence posts, bricks, and garden boxes.

in a foil strip affixed to the frame below it: I HOPE YOU LOVE BIRDS TOO. IT'S ECONOMICAL. IT SAVES GOING TO HEAVEN. Now hurry back to the garden with those images still burning in the mind's eye and imagine that you've entered the collage box, that in fact you're part of the composition, a stray figure caught between painted sky and wooden fence post. A child's game, true, but a valuable one to play here.

Another game worth playing in Nitzke Marquis's garden is to pretend you're a bird hovering fifty or sixty feet above the property. The bird's-eye view reveals much about the way she and her husband, renowned glass artist Richard Marquis, use structures, garden boxes, fences, trees, and grassy areas to shape their landscape. Around the fence that frames the artichoke heart of garden boxes they have set another, looser frame, a grassy field edged with sheds and house; and this compound in its turn is girdled by a grove of cedars and firs, the whole composition crowning the brow of a high, fair hillside overlooking Puget Sound and the Olympic Mountains. Theirs is a makeshift, provisional approach to landscape architecture: gentle, informal, unobtrusive yet grounded in utility.

This is a landscape made over to suit the needs and the tastes of working artists. The outbuildings, which appear at first glance to be farm sheds or funky dormitories, are actually studios where the pair toil away making beautiful, intriguing things out of glass (in his case) and out of everything under the sun plus glass (in hers). The whole place has the aura of a paradisiacal summer camp devoted to priming the imagination. A bucolic art factory. A workshop of the creative spirit. The second you lay eyes on the eight-foot pyramid of bowling balls that rises at the entrance to the property, you know you're leaving the "real" world behind and entering a realm where very different rules apply.

Left: Gas and roses: The "Red Crown Gasoline" sign is an unlikely companion for an exuberant spray of 'Golden Wings' rambler roses, but it works in this garden.

Right: Nitzke Marquis's studio sits like an enchanted woodland hut in a shady nook outside the garden fence.

Lanky, fair, freckled, her blue eyes glowing behind pale lashes, her long reddish hair pulled back and braided, Nitzke Marquis has a calm, capable, attentive air, as if she's always got one ear cocked for the whisperings of inspiration. Inspiration in the studio or out under the fickle Northwest sky: it all ultimately wells up from the same source. When you spend even a few hours in her company, you come to understand that gardening is not a hobby for her or an outlet for excess energy: it's as essential as her art. She gardens by instinct, by strong inclination, and by heritage. In the Wisconsin dairy country where she was born and raised, gardens tended to be big and useful—planted more for food than for show—and she retains some of that no-nonsense respect for the fundamentals. Hers is a working garden that is expected to produce and perform: plants that don't measure up, need coddling, exhaust her interest, or prove distracting soon fall by the wayside. At least half of the space is devoted to fruits and vegetables—mizuna, leeks, apples, berries, and the potatoes she adores—but the food-bearing plants are intermingled with the flowers and placed with the same sharp attention to texture, color, shape, and cultural requirements. Campanula and chard, a change purse and a glass potato, raspberry and rose, jars and embroidered buttons: they are all elements of equal value in Nitzke Marquis's eclectic compositions.

After attending the University of Wisconsin at Madison during the tumultuous 1960s ("Mad Town," they called it then), Johanna Nitzke lit out for the West Coast, first to San Francisco, then to Olympia, Washington, to attend Evergreen State College, then up to Alaska for a spell, and finally down to Seattle, where she worked as Public Art Director for Washington State and then landed the position of director of the Foster-White Gallery. It was there, in 1987, that she met glass artist Richard Marquis, whom she married less than three months later. Lots of things happened quickly at this juncture in her life. After the marriage, the couple moved into a partially finished cedar house on a five-acre parcel that Marquis already owned (they soon added five more acres). Within

two months, even before the house was completed, Nitzke Marquis had begun on her garden—not just mapping but actually digging and installing.

In choosing which plants to add to the composition, Nitzke Marquis has always worked from intuition, association, idiosyncratic preferences, and sheer whimsy. Plants must have history—and so her boxes are full of familiar traditional flowers such as

achillea, lupine, hollyhock, columbine, rose, poppy, daisy. They must have folklore associated with them, they must remind her of someplace or something she loves, they must have literary resonance, they must reflect one of her current passions (just now hostas are in, fuchsias definitely on their way out), they must thrive in her garden (no idiosyncrasy here). Take the potato. In this garden, the humble tuber has been liberated from dull utilitarian rows and turned into a centerpiece, a foreground star, a delicately mounded companion to the digitalis, forget-me-nots, hollyhocks, and edible Asian green mizuna. In her overflowing boxes Nitzke Marquis has enshrined the potato as an edible thing of beauty. Potato as food. Potato as landmark on the garden calendar ("They must go into the ground on St. Paddy's Day!"). Potato as heritage ("I always enjoyed digging potatoes as a child growing up in Wisconsin"). Potato as form (who ever noticed how decorative their juicy green articulated leaves are, especially as a frothy foreground to hollyhock spires?). Potato as object (in one of her recent "botanical tributes," Nitzke Marquis has taken knobby brown glass potatoes blown by her husband and placed them inside an antique botanist's collection case—early botanists, with their zeal for amassing and sorting plant specimens, are her soul mates). Potato as desirable plant in every way. The meanings and reasons for each plant proliferate the longer you contemplate.

"Only connect!" That resounding imperative out of E. M. Forster might be a fitting motto for this garden. Only connect— art and garden, memory and history, sustenance and association. In Nitzke Marquis's garden and in her art, the delicious brown-skinned lump becomes a kind of symbol of the world—a wry, whimsical symbol whose meanings take root and spread in many directions. And there are scores of other such symbols lurking beside the ferns, nodding next

Left: Only collect: Rummage sale finds look right at home amid Nitzke Marquis's living collage of lupines, chives, leeks, and potatoes.

Right: Nitzke Marquis nestled this imposing vase by glass artist Dante Marioni in a thicket of hollyhocks, foxgloves, and leeks.

to the calendulas, hiding in the old roses, flickering under the drifts of the 'Nora Barlow' columbine cherished by Gertrude Jekyll—connections waiting to be teased out and followed back to her art, her reading, her latest passion. Nitzke Marquis's is a subtle, quirky, low-key garden that yields up its secrets slowly and in surprising ways. This is a not a garden of perfection where every stem and vine has been clipped and staked into submission; nor is it a garden of Zen-like simplicity where a single spray of blossom quivers serenely over the hardscape. Rather, like the art that happens in the sheds and studios all around—collage-making, glass-making, painting, collecting and sifting and combining odd objects—it is a work in progress, a thing that may never be entirely finished but is completely and intensely itself at any given moment.

Though this garden is emphatically Nitzke Marquis's one-woman show, her husband very much makes his presence felt here. To begin with, there is lots of wonderful glass in the garden. Those candy-bright glass cones capping the fence posts are color tests from Dick's studio, a reminder that art happens, as gardening itself does, by trial and error. That oversize vase nestled in with the holly-hocks, foxgloves, and leeks—a chest-high fabrication consisting of a fire-engine-red urn topped by a flaring trumpet of Easter-chick yellow—is the work of Dick Marquis's friend and collaborator, glass artist Dante Marioni. Marquis also had a hand in the planning and construction of what surely qualifies as the ultimate garden ornament—a towering eight-foot pyramid of over 1,800 bowling balls stacked on a concrete platform at the entrance to the compound (Johanna and Dick begged and filched from friends and haunted Goodwill stores). What do you plant around a bowling-ball pyramid? Ferns, of course, and astilbe and Solomon's seal and bits of sweet woodruff to play off the curtain of surrounding cedar and dawn redwood. It makes quite a statement as you turn into the driveway—a statement one might decipher as something like "Abandon all preconceptions about art and gardening, ye who enter here." In fact, this bowling-ball pyramid, like its predecessors in Egypt, is a tomb: the ashes of a beloved dog rest beneath. It is

also a perfect illustration of how artists can transform familiar materials by using them in entirely new ways. In a garden, in a collage, or in a box, objects may not be what you think they are. When you take two artists as multiply talented as Dick and Johanna and set them down together on ten inspiring acres, art happens in all sorts of strange and unexpected ways, inside and out.

Artists who garden usually end up in one camp or other—the plant camp or the object/structure camp—but Nitzke Marquis manages to have a foot in each without conflict. One of her secrets of survival is that she nurses only one or two plant (or plant-family) passions per season. A few years ago it was clematis, and after months of study, reading, catalogue-flipping, and daydreaming, she felt she knew enough to begin to plant. Now the luxuriant vines fill her garden, winding happily through trees, trellises, and other plants (especially striking is the *Clematis montana* 'Elizabeth' weaving into the climbing rose 'Kiftsgate' on a tall lattice affixed to the house). Next came a lily-and-columbine phase. After that it was hostas—"Much to my horror," she confides with a grimace. "They are the ultimate challenge here in slug country. Slugs come from other counties to find our hostas. But still, I wanted hostas and I wanted to see them next to Solomon's seal. Both are so understated by nature."

Strangely, given how much she knows about plants and how well she grows them, Nitzke Marquis insists that she's less interested in the plants themselves than in their shape and silhouette and their place in the overall composition. "Shape" and "circumference" are words she uses repeatedly: "I'm obsessive about the shapes of things. My interest is related to periphery and what the eye sees on the outside, and with that comes spontaneous combustion that makes the whole picture. The circumference: what makes

Left: Even before the cedar house was finished, Nitzke Marquis began mapping, digging, and installing her garden.

Right: *Clematis* 'Nelly Moser', white wisteria, and swelling peony buds fill this corner of the garden with fleeting, harmonious early summer color.

a thing a whole is what you're looking around. If I put a plant in a space, it's what's around it that makes it wonderful. I'm concerned with what the eye sees overall rather than specifics. 'My Business is Circumference,' Emily Dickinson wrote somewhere. That clicks with me."

Many of the shapes in Nitzke Marquis's garden are subtle—spears of white campanula punctuating the bubbling curls of lettuce and spinach, volunteer columbines raising jagged profiles against the slats of the fence. Others are quite bold, even over-the-top. The enormous crimp-edged fronds of an immense *Gunnera* cast an aura of tropical excess over the corner of the garden closest to the house. (This South American giant looks smashing from the upstairs window and from the kitchen window, where it is the first thing the eye falls on.) Dante Marioni's vase lends a cartoonish, Brobdingnagian touch to the corner it occupies. The 'Etoile de Holland' rose that clambers over Nitzke Marquis's studio is exuberant to the point of excess. And of course the bowling ball pyramid is in a class by itself as far as high drama goes.

As for perimeter, Nitzke Marquis had a jump on this design element from the start in the strong outlines of her boxes and the fence that surrounds them. (Both, by the way, also serve practical purposes: the boxes raised the plantings four to six inches above the flood-prone hardpan, and the fence keeps out the bumptious family dog, who in turn is charged with warding off deer and chipmunks.) Nitzke Marquis has chosen to boldface some of these outlines with unusual or striking materials: unpeeled cedar half-logs give the sides of her boxes texture and heft, while striking white Victorian garden tiles decorated with a running braid pattern frame a healthy stand of raspberries and marionberries in flea-market chic. Oddness turns up in trellising materials as well: near the center of the garden Nitzke Marquis has set up two laundry-drying

Left: The interior of Nitzke Marquis's studio is a work of collage art in its own right.

Right: Johanna Nitzke Marquis at the main gate to her fenced garden.

racks as supports for her pole beans, and elsewhere she has propped old wooden ladders (acquired at garage sales) against trees—an inventive and inexpensive way to trellis rambler roses.

Nitzke Marquis also brings the written word to the garden. An inscription placed within range of an inviting, sun-dappled, wisteria-scented chair forces one to sit still at least long enough to read the words and muse over their meaning. "When the world wearies and society ceases to function there is always the garden." Inscriptions turn up in Nitzke Marquis's art as well, and for much the same reason: words encourage the viewer to look again, revise one's first impression, find new meanings, seize new inspiration. Words bounce off images to spark those all-important connections. So, on a botanical tribute to Gertrude Jekyll, Nitzke Marquis has copied out this quote from John Ruskin: "The path of a good woman is indeed strewn with flowers, but they rise behind her steps not before them."

Nitzke Marquis elaborates on this theme as she wanders down her own garden path through artful living collages of *Linaria*, allium, poppy, and lupine: "The abundance is overwhelming—that is the joy of it. Where else can you be in the midst of such abundance? We live in this abundance in the garden and nowhere else. When you make a garden, there is a natural progression from abundance to selection. You feel you must grow everything to begin with, and then you become Zen-like."

This is the essence of her approach both in the studio and outside among her garden boxes: she savors and celebrates the abundance and then figures out how to manage and contain it. In a word: discipline. The discipline to select the exact right button or miniature frog statue from the galaxies of objects she keeps on hand and then to find a place for it inside (or on) the ornate antique frame she has restored; the discipline to zero in on just one plant group —hostas, clematis —and bring multitudes of them to perfection in a single season. The discipline to divide her time fruitfully between her garden and her art, so that each realm complements and cross-pollinates the other.

As Nitzke Marquis would be the first to point out, the lessons of art and the lessons of gardening are essentially the same: "When is a piece of art done? When is it enough weeding? The trick is to know when to let it go and let the garden or the art work through you."

The Artist's Eye

Words in the Garden: Nitzke Marquis tucks inscriptions, mottoes, and whimsical signs ("Cut flowers for sale") away in odd corners of her garden for inspiration, comic relief, or simply as reminders to slow down, rest, muse, and remember. She uses unique materials to create signs—old boards, mosaics, painted rulers—hand-lettering them or hammering in metallic letters for a rustic effect. An eclectic reader, Nitzke Marquis draws on enduring favorite passages for her inscriptions. Whenever one enters the garden gate, the eye falls on these beloved words inscribed on a venerable yardstick: "Every garden is an act of hope."

Creative Boxing, Fencing, and Containing: Most of us think of garden boxes as structures to hold plants and fences as protection for what lies within, but Nitzke Marquis permits—indeed, encourages—her garden to overflow, wind around, hide and recline against her containers. Drifts of peonies, poppies, forget-me-nots, and columbines have sprung up outside her main garden fence, suggesting the unruly vitality of what lies within. More columbines, lilies, and Japanese anemones look lovely with the fence slats as background and support. Nitzke Marquis's boxes and fences become important design elements in their own right, not simply utilitarian devices for organizing the garden. Even the monstrous *Gunnera* is raised up in a whiskey barrel—accented, yet contained.

Mixing Vegetables and Flowers: For some reason, most of us practice a strict segregation policy when it comes to growing vegetables and ornamental plants. Nitzke Marquis has done wonders by tossing out the stodgy old rule and mixing leeks and hollyhocks, mizuna and sweet peas, spinach and calendulas. Of course, she pays attention to the cultural needs of the plants and also to practical considerations like bloom/fruiting time and ease of harvest. Potatoes and roses just wouldn't get along in the same bed, and Nitzke Marquis doesn't try to force them to. But she does have a grand time experimenting with new combinations of color, texture, size, leaf variety, and degree of edibility. She fully exploits the ornamental qualities of the edibles by juxtaposing lettuce and roses, spinach and daisies, sunflowers and potatoes. And it certainly makes the lettuce harvest more pleasant when you can inhale sweet peas as you pick.

Still Lifes and Shrines in the Garden: Nitzke Marquis enlivens her garden with striking vignettes—small still lifes composed of plants, pottery, signs, symbols, unusual pots, and found objects. On a cedar panel fixed to the side of the house she has created a little study in geometric forms: a disc-shaped white plaster bas-relief of daffodils is mounted above two white plaster fleur-de-lys plant shelves holding tiny pots of spring flowers; centered beneath the pots, a large orange glass globe rises like a smooth sun out of a thicket of campanula stalks. It's just an odd corner of the garden, but Nitzke Marquis has worked her magic on it, transforming it into a petite surrealist shrine—to whatever divinity one chooses. Similarly, two white floral-patterned Victorian plates mounted on slats of the fence flank a small basket stuck with a few columbine stems: a tribute to the prettiest flowers of the moment. There's even a whimsical automotive shrine: an old barnlike structure carries the crayon-red Pegasus that was once the symbol of Mobil gasoline as well as a Red Crown gasoline sign—with a splendid yellow rambler rose climbing out of a box beneath.

Design and Neglect:
The Garden of Arthur Erickson

If, by some chance, the plain planked cedar gate had been left open to the quiet side street in Vancouver, British Columbia, and you couldn't resist the urge to step through it, you'd never guess in a million years that you had come upon the garden and house of Arthur Erickson, Canada's premier architect. Indeed, you might not realize that you were in a garden at all. Vegetation runs riot in every direction. Rhodies the size of station wagons collide with thickets of grasses, bamboo, laurel. A huge

Douglas fir, that most common and most characteristic Northwest tree, shades masses of ordinary Northwest salal, huckleberry, vine maple. In front of you and to the left, a vague clearing opens in front of a low structure that could be a garage or perhaps a studio. A dozen or so yards from the building there's a glint of water: a pond (or is it two or three ponds?), all but smothered in rushes, water lilies, iris, and moss—lots and lots of moss. And on every side, fences covered in dense foliage so effectively screen out the surrounding houses of the quiet, rather ordinary residential neighborhood near the University of British Columbia that you forget where you are, how you got here, how you're going to get out.

This tangle, this chaos, this *mess* is the garden of Arthur Erickson? *The* Arthur Erickson? The internationally renowned creator of the soaring glass and concrete Museum of Anthropology at the University of British Columbia, the magnificent multilevel Robson Square complex of law courts and government buildings in downtown Vancouver, the campus of Simon Fraser University? The designer whose hallmarks are waterfalls, cascades of steps, massive volumes that seem to hover in midair, austere swaths of clear ground set off by soft, light-catching textures?

The answer is that all the elements of Erickson's style are, in essence, here—you just have to learn how to see them. To see what's going on in this extraordinary garden you need to relax and settle in. Shed your preconceptions of what a garden is and isn't. Surrender to the quirky spirit of the place. In fact, this is not a mess at all, but a subtle and original creation—a true artist's garden that was launched with a firm, affectionate, if rather haphazard, shove, and then left to fend for itself. In Arthur Erickson's quirky collaboration with nature, nature has definitely been granted the upper hand.

A dapper, finely knit man with blue eyes much younger looking than his lined, handsome face and full head of gray hair, Erickson fashioned this garden out of a combination of pressing necessity, serendipity, whim, and blind faith. When he bought the property (for a song) in 1957, there was a traditional English-style cottage garden—delphiniums, lupines, phlox, rose arbor, white picket fence—spread out on a narrow, deep (120- by 66-foot) lot with two garages and a kind of lean-to structure occupying an 18-foot-deep band at the far north end. Erickson was at a stage of his career when he was on the road almost constantly, so he simply let the garden slide. As for the buildings, rather than construct a conventional house in the center of the lot as his neighbors expected him to do, Erickson ingeniously knit together the old garages and lean-to by removing most of the dividing walls and partitions, building a central skylit "bridge" section for a new kitchen and bathroom, and adding sliding doors, mirrored entryways, and a small greenhouse opening out onto a brick terrace and the garden beyond. The 1,200-square-foot house is unobtrusive on the site and as seemingly artless as the garden: the hipped and gable roofs keep a low profile, the surrounding shrubs of privet and camellia hide much of the structure, and it's situated so far back on the lot that one barely notices it upon entering and rarely glimpses it from the garden.

"Architecturally this house is so terrible that I would never admit to being here," Erickson once told an interviewer with characteristic sly self-deprecation. Actually, the house harmonizes wonderfully with the garden, framing soothingly deep and bright views from all its many south-facing windows and sliding doors. Erickson strongly believes that architecture is "not a statement but a response" to a given site, and his own house, which of course is anything but "terrible," is a perfect illustration of this principle. The house is in a sense a garden room with walls of glass rather than of shrubbery.

Erickson loves to tell the tale of how his present garden rose on the wreckage of the original English cottage borders. "I thought the place could be self-sufficient, but the catch was that someone had to take care of all that. The second year it became like a deserted

Right: "Only after burying what had been an English border garden beneath a high mound of earth did I recognize that the character of the site was that of a forest clearing," Erickson remarks of his garden.

garden. It was terribly romantic, the kind of secret garden that children love—saturated with weeds but with the flowers still growing and the grass a foot high. The third year, the weeds took over entirely, so I got a bulldozer and told the operator to bury the garden, dig a hole, and make a hill high enough so I couldn't see the house across the street. . . . I had to get rid of that view."

The present garden evolved from this earth-moving undertaking in 1960. As Erickson wrote in his second book, *The Architecture of Arthur Erickson* (1988), "The act of recognition is not always easy. In my own garden, for example, only after burying what had been an English border garden beneath a high mound of earth did I recognize that the character of the site was that of a forest clearing." The mound that got pushed up left a large, gaping hole in the center of the property; Erickson hired a student to lay down roofing paper and add water—and voilà, he had a small, shallow, naturalistic pond as a highlight in the "forest clearing." "I have never touched or cleaned this pond since," insists Erickson today—and it looks it.

For plants, rather than spend a lot on exotic ornamentals at nurseries, he went to the Fraser River estuary and the Endowment Lands of the University of British Columbia and dug out grasses and rushes and shore pines that caught his eye (not a recommended approach, and in any case, illegal on public lands in the States). Erickson is very fond of one native grass (he's terrible with plant names) whose stalks tend to break in the wind "so you get this nice line." Most gardeners are terrified of bamboo—with reason—but Erickson liked it and had room for it, so he went wild creating a bamboo forest of ten different species, predominantly golden and dwarf variegated, at the far end of the pond. (He has come

Left: The Japanese holly in the foreground is one of the only shrubs that Erickson prunes – it adds "some discipline to the rank disorder," he notes.

Right: Erickson's house, as viewed from the mound. One would never guess from inside Erickson's garden how dense and suburban the surrounding neighborhood is.

to regret that choice and now jokes, "I keep hoping the bamboo will grow old and die before I do.") Zebra grass *(Miscanthus sinensis zebrinus)* appealed to him, so he massed it in big rustling clumps that reach ten feet by midsummer. A couple of fruit trees and a dogwood survived from the old garden, and Erickson added a persimmon tree that has grown up into a wonderfully tortured piece of arboreal sculpture near the house. The only really pricey plants on the property are a grove of rare Himalayan rhododendrons that arrived as gifts from landscape-gardener friends. Once the major

divisions of space and the large groupings of plants were in place, "I just let the whole thing go," says Erickson.

That's the story he loves to tell, but of course it's only part of the story. For you can't just let any garden go, as Erickson discovered with the property's original English cottage garden. You have to know how to work in partnership with nature, choose plants that will naturalize attractively, and anticipate how they will change and blend with each other over the years. Above all, you have to have an underlying structure that's strong enough to survive being

"let go." That's where it helps to be an architect, and helps supremely to be an architect as sensitive to challenging sites as Arthur Erickson is. He once told an interviewer, "I tend to take a structural approach to landscape and a landscape approach to architecture," and it certainly shows, both in his own garden and in the Robson Square complex, where the tiers of concrete are thickly swathed—indeed, almost buried—in foliage and flowing water. Erickson has written that the twin *allées* of trees that line Robson Square "remain my favourite design contribution to the city's

streets." "I have a good eye," he says frankly, "I know when something is right, though I can't always give the reason."

The eye: that's exactly where his garden design begins. The pond is one shining example. Erickson's "eye" led him to a limited palette of mostly native plants that would look good together and that would grow happily, if sometimes a bit awkwardly, without pruning or summer watering. To the soft, irregular shape scooped out by the bulldozer, Erickson added a rectangular travertine marble "moon-viewing" platform that slopes down gently into the water. (The original travertine slab, which had been salvaged from the remodel of the men's bathroom at the Hotel Vancouver, was recently replaced with more durable Brazilian granite.) So, to begin with, there's the rhythm of straight and curving lines, and the interplay of two horizontal surfaces—one made of water, the other of stone and cement. Then Erickson planted the perimeter of the platform with easy low-maintenance plants in harmonizing textures and shapes: gracefully curving bladed and stalky plants like chives, ornamental grasses, and iris; bristling clumps of Alberta spruce and looser mounds of yellow potentilla; a bold contrasting accent contributed by a *Tibouchina urvilleana*—a Brazilian shrub with brilliant royal purple flowers and open growth. Around the pond itself he interspersed ordinary small-leafed groundcovers like ajuga and creeping jenny with the splashy reflective green banners of a native skunk cabbage, and he knit the pattern together with humps of salal. Over the years moss and tiny native ferns have staged a heavy invasion, painting all exposed horizontal surfaces near the pond in glowing deep-green velvet.

What he has achieved by blending austere, elemental structure with freely doodled plantings is a superbly casual composition—a man-made approximation of one of those gemlike glens you occasionally stumble upon deep in the forest, where every leaf and stalk and rock and bit of open ground takes its place in a wonderfully accidental but perfectly harmonious pattern. In arriving at this state of pleasing disorder, placement is essential: Erickson's initial plantings were made with an eye to creating a series of gently curved horizontals that run through the garden rather than showing off choice specimens. Here and there a single tree—like the persimmon near the hot tub—got special attention in order to fix the character of a space. Once the lines were drawn and the areas defined, Erickson stood back and let serendipity, chance, luck, and benign neglect take over. Time and nature have blurred the lines, but not erased them: the garden still makes a strong visual statement as *garden* rather than abandoned lot because the solid, naturalistic structure was in place at the start.

One trademark of Erickson's architecture is a sense of limitless lightness: his buildings, even the enormous public buildings like the UBC Museum of Anthropology, appear to hover over their sites and disappear into their landscapes. His buildings seem to materialize out of thin air and fade back into it at some indefinite vanishing point deep in space. There's a counterpoint between grandeur and humility in an Erickson structure: his houses, refusing to puncture the skyline, are rarely visible from the street, yet they seem to soar as you approach them; his public buildings lack the spotlit, triumphal entries, towers, columns, or ornaments of traditional and postmodern buildings, yet they beckon the passerby to pause, study their planes and angles, follow the flow of lines in and up and around them.

The same fundamental design principles apply in the garden, though on a smaller scale, from a slyer perspective. As Erickson muses, looking out from the deck around his house at the plant-dappled sheet of water, "I always want to make space appear larger than it is. The secret is to hide the end—conceal the end of a beam or the termination of a fence. It has to disappear—this makes it more interesting." To create and enhance a sense of depth in this relatively small lot, Erickson has played brilliantly with horizontals: "You put as

Left: The moon-viewing platform, recently redone in Brazilian granite and raised slightly, is the most emphatic horizontal in a garden of horizontals.

Right: A study in form and texture: Solomon's seal (*Polygonatum* x *hybridum*) and maidenhair fern contrast with the rough mossy stone of Erickson's "Stonehenge."

many horizontal planes, one in front of another, within your field of vision as possible. There is a series of layers back through the property, and the more detail you put into your view, the more it extends the distance." Erickson's horizontals are not usually rigidly rectilinear planes but rather smooth flowing billows muffled by moss. The mound adds a sense of mystery: what is behind it? The pond sets up a psychological divide: one is compelled to cross the water, even if only visually, and arrive at another "land" on the opposite shore.

Again, what appears at first glance to be a pleasing tangle of foliage, water, and hardscape turns out to be a painstaking manipulation of space. In fact, Erickson points to exactly twelve planes running from the house back to the southern property line: the deck; the low clipped hedge; the brick walkway past the hedge; the moon-viewing platform by the water; the water itself; the mass of rushes and grasses; the "beach" on the far side; the pines and above them the junipers that merge into an irregular horizontal on the mound; the bamboo forest; the dogwood and fir; and the rippling sheet of Lombardy poplars at the far end.

Erickson is emphatically not a plantsman, a fact that becomes apparent as you stroll through the garden with him and listen to his stories and reminiscences. When questioned about his favorite parts of the garden or how he integrated the plantings around the pool, he tends to respond instead with yarns such as the one about the raccoons that invaded the premises to feast on the gorgeous carp ("pale, pale metallic gold that glistened") he had released into the pool. His endeavor to get rid of the furry pests eventually embroiled Erickson and a friend of his in a midnight ambush of a treed raccoon that woke the entire neighborhood and brought a squadron of police cars to the garden gate. Next he tried

Left: The ponds that lace Erickson's garden act as both horizontal planes and mirrors for the surrounding plants.

Right: Moss, uninivited but welcome through-out the garden, provides a backdrop for this composition in rock, stalk, and shadow.

stocking the pond with elegant, black-feathered red-beaked Australian swans borrowed from the Vancouver Zoo. The swans were paddling gracefully amid the grasses and bamboo shadows the night that the Royal Ballet came for a party. "The Ballet was doing *Swan Lake*," he recalls, "and when the dancers saw the swans, the boys and girls stripped and jumped in. There were many distinguished Vancouverites there—a rather uptight crowd—but they all took it quite calmly."

For Erickson, the garden is not so much a precious work of art or a shrine to his most sacred beliefs as a place to unwind (when

he's not entertaining)—a green hideout where he can relax, screen out the world and commune with nature. "It's the visual quiet that I appreciate," he remarks. "There's a certain serenity and tranquillity here—enormous calm. Everything has adjusted to what is next to it. There is a relationship, an accommodation."

Erickson acknowledges the influence of traditional garden-design techniques—notably Japanese and Italian—but he has characteristically bent long-established practices and rules to suit his own needs. He learned from the Japanese to exclude straight lines and to use "borrowed scenery," although because his garden is fenced and hedged on all sides he borrows only the tops of neighboring trees, a feature that contributes to the sense of limitless "country" space. According to Erickson, Chinese gardens gave him the idea of confining colorful flowers to a single grouping of containers. And, sure enough, on a patio near the house there is a little ghetto of vivid bloom. The riot of clashing hues he has nursed up in a hodgepodge of terra-cotta and plastic flower pots looks more Bohemian than Chinese. Erickson claims he visits the local Safeway at the start of every summer and grabs whatever catches his eye: red nicotiana and orange geranium, blue lobelia, blue and pink and red petunias. "I like them mixed and crowded indiscriminately," he says, "everything fighting for its life." Crowning this collection of brazen annuals is a fuchsia-flowered zonal geranium that Erickson has allowed to grow fantastically tall and leggy—a kind of ghostly, gangly, sun-starved mutant cousin to the pert, bushy geraniums most of us keep.

Erickson is rather proud of how little he contributes to the care or maintenance of the garden. There is no watering or deadheading; plants that don't make it die and disappear; volunteer madronas have been allowed to grow undisturbed. The garden is "planned so as to keep a certain discipline," he

Left: In late afternoon, the "floating fence" that runs along the east property line becomes a screen for ever-changing shadow pictures cast by overhanging bamboo.

Right: Arthur Erickson in the garden he created more than forty years ago.

told an interviewer. "Otherwise, it would do too well in this wet climate." But Erickson is not quite as aloof from the evolution of the garden as he likes to appear. Though most plants have been "let go," there is some selective pruning. Near the house, a large slab of Japanese holly with tight, tiny, curled leaves is precisely squared off and shaved flat on top, rather like boxwood, to pick up the rectilinear pattern of the redwood deck (it provides "some discipline to the rank disorder," says Erickson); a shell-pink camellia is also clipped to present a geometric form against the house façade.

Somehow, despite his international reputation, Erickson got into serious financial difficulties in the early 1990s—he actually had to declare bankruptcy—and very nearly lost his house and garden to the three mortgageholders who were waiting in the wings to foreclose and sell the place to developers. (The property was by then valued at $825,000 in Canadian dollars.) In 1992, supporters of Erickson in Vancouver's design and architecture community launched a movement to save the property, and finally in 1997 they succeeded in buying it through a foundation set up with generous grants from architect and philanthropist Phyllis Lambert, founder of the Canadian Centre for Architecture in Montreal, and Vancouver real estate developer Peter Wall. The Arthur Erickson House and Garden Foundation allows Erickson to live here as long as he wants to, but he technically no longer owns the property.

In a sense, Erickson's garden—like all gardens made with care and thought and need—is an extension of himself, an expression of his deepest, perhaps even unconscious, ideas on art and nature and our place in both. It is a humble, messy, unimposing green laboratory in which he studies how a site changes and evolves over time and how a landscape grows around and with and sometimes through a house. "I am an observer, not an intruder, in the garden," Erickson insists. "It is endlessly fascinating to see what it will produce."

The Artist's Eye

The Artful Uses of Illusion:
"Illusion is everywhere" in this garden, wrote Edith Iglauer in a profile of Erickson published in *The New Yorker* in 1979. "The lake is actually an artfully placed pond deep enough to contain fish, and the mountain is an eight-foot mound of earth." Erickson has carefully created the illusion of depth on his lot by layering materials, placing horizontal planes one behind another, and camouflaging the property line. The effect, notes Iglauer, is to give the illusion of "spacious, lovely country landscape continuing into the beyond." Erickson also plays with perspective and scale: a clump of untended bamboo has grown tall and dense enough to feel like a jungle; the placement of two rocks (often visited by ducks and cranes) on the moon-viewing platform draws the eye down to the minuscule mounds of moss and fairylike ferns that have grown on and around it; the wildness of the grasses and shrubs makes them appear bigger than they really are.

Setting a Mood with the Garden Entrance:
As an architect, Erickson is acutely aware of how we perceive space and how we perceive the transition in "feeling" as we move from street to garden. In his own garden, he has enhanced the mystery of this transition by erecting a high fence facing the street—so high, so thickly draped with ivy that it entirely hides the house and nearly all of the garden save a huge Douglas fir and a vigorous laurel. Where is the entrance? Even when you spot what must be a gate, you're still not sure how to enter or whether anyone will respond to the feeble sounds emitted by the simple, weathered bronze Japanese knocker in the form of a chrysanthemum (symbol of rest and ease and contemplation). When the gate swings open into the garden, you notice a rough, raised-stone threshold such as might mark the entrance to a Japanese tea garden. In forcing you to stop and step over it, this threshold marks a point of transition. Once you clear the threshold, you find yourself on a stepping-stone path that proceeds through thickets of huckleberry and vine maple to the deck. In just a few steps, the entrance has worked its magic and enveloped you in a different world.

Creative Fencing:
Enclosure is crucial to Erickson's garden design: he wanted a space that would be a world unto itself, a world invisible from the street and free of the distractions of surrounding houses and yards. The obvious way of creating enclosure is through fencing or hedging, but he ran into a problem with local ordinances: the city of Vancouver permitted only a four-foot-high fence on the east property line. That was not high enough to suit him, so Erickson came up with an ingenious solution: he built the fence to local code, planted a line of clumping "fountain" bamboo (*Arundinaria nitida*) along the fence, and then constructed a kind of suspended screen inside the fence that has the effect of "sandwiching" the bamboo between two graceful horizontal wooden structures. From inside the garden what you see is a seemingly endless horizontal panel of cedar slats "floating" two feet off the ground in front of the bamboo. The suspended fence provides total privacy and crops the view of the bamboo in an interesting way: the stems have formed an impenetrable living mat at the bottom, and every afternoon as the sun sinks, the floating panel itself becomes a kind of canvas displaying the intricate, ever-changing patterns of the bamboo fronds waving at the top.

Uncontrolled but Not Chaotic:
Erickson has pushed the notion of the "low-maintenance" garden to its limit—and beyond—yet the result is not chaos but a subtle and fluid melding of art and nature. The secret of why this works so well is structure. To start with, he let the major structural divisions be dictated by utility. Once he had established the big spaces within his clearing, he "filled" them in sparingly and instinctively with a limited palette of plants. Ornamental grasses are planted in configurations that create "rooms" as the summer progresses. A few clumps of water irises with tiny blue flowers stand out as waterside focal points. Azaleas near the pond send up masses of cotton-candy-pink flowers for a few weeks in spring, but for the rest of the year they stabilize and soften the bank and draw a loose, pleasing margin between pond and "forest."

Far left: The classical columns and lush colors of this water feature set the mood for the garden of sculptors George Little and David Lewis.

Left: Painted concrete casts of exotic leaves are a Little and Lewis trademark.

The Uses of Enchantment:

The Exotically Classical Garden of George Little and David Lewis

Fantasy makes all gardens grow. Without it you may have yard, plot, park, grounds, but you lack the essential ingredient of garden, the element that seizes the imagination and transports or envelops you into a world invented by the gardener. But of course some gardens are more fantastic than others, and a very few are so fantastic that they seem to be more about fantasy than about gardening. Like a play within a play, these gardens comment on the nature of illusion, the mechanics of mesmerization, the mystery of why and how the simple act of cordoning off space and time can charge them so highly with meaning.

On a third of an acre on Bainbridge Island, a short ferry ride across Puget Sound from downtown Seattle, sculptors and painters George Little and David Lewis have created one of these rare fantastic gardens. The street is ordinary, the house pleasant

Below: A single *Macleaya cordata* leaf floats on a lens of water in a surreal hemispheric rain basin fashioned by Little and Lewis.

Right: George Little (left) and David Lewis (right) work together on many of their sculptures and commissions and sign their work jointly.

but unremarkable, the grounds small and flat, but together these two art-and-garden collaborators have managed to distill the elixir of garden fantasy. Frothy with outsize tropical foliage, vivid with the sound and gleam of flowing water, riotous with colors quite alien to the mushroomy tones of the Northwest, the Little and Lewis garden is the perfect showcase for the ancient-looking columns, fountains, basins, wall plaques, and furniture for which these artists are becoming increasingly and justly renowned. It's garden as stage set for a Lewis Carrollesque mad tea party in Roman-Mexican drag.

The spell begins to work the moment you set foot on their property, or even before. As you approach their driveway, the eye falls on a tiny rectangular sign—"Little and Lewis, by appointment only" in sky-blue letters—hugged by a lime-green clump of lady's mantle and shadowed by one of their signature column capitals sporting a topknot of variegated blue flag iris. Deeper within the tangle gleams the aerial cascade of a mature golden chain tree in glorious bloom. All sorts of odd and disparate associations begin to hum and tick in the mind: Mexican hacienda, Portuguese courtyard, Pompeian wall painting, Minoan pottery, saturated swaths of Rothko colors. Take two giant steps and you find yourself transported from chromatic whimsy to sublime architectural cleverness: on the left side of the drive a rank of faded, washed blue and green columns, each a different height and set with different shapes and textures of plants, rises from a long, low, rectangular pool of dark shallow water framed in a low terra-cotta–colored wall. Though this water feature—one of many in the garden—is not large, something about the profile of the columns against the stuccoed wall, the scale of the composition, the crisply etched vividness of individual plants, and the richly exotic colors conjures up the sense of deep space and ancient time. It's as if a fragment of a Roman villa, miraculously suffused with wonderful new colors, had surfaced on Bainbridge Island. Or maybe as if a capsule of brilliant Mediterranean weather and light had been imported and preserved intact from the surrounding weepy gray. Somehow the

collision of climatic illusion with temporal and geographical illusion makes you instantly cheerful, lighthearted, and intensely curious to see more.

It comes as no surprise after even the briefest acquaintance with their garden and their art that David Lewis and George Little both love archaeology (Lewis even freelanced for a while in Greece as an archaeological illustrator). In fact, love of ancient ruins was part of what inspired this remarkable partnership in the first place. "We went to Greece together in 1992," explains Lewis, "discovered we have a lot in common, and have been collaborating ever since." Their first joint project was a small fountain, a commission that came while both were supporting themselves by working at a Bainbridge bakery. After three years, on the strength of several more commissions, they quit the bakery and started a business of putting in garden pools, which lasted a little more than a year. "It was basically ditchdigging," recalls Lewis. "Definitely not for you if your real passion is sculpting."

Their easygoing, fluid, artistic partnership is in many ways a fusing of opposites. Lewis—intense, wiry, dark, moustached, plainspoken—is Midwestern by birth, a graduate of Oberlin College, and a veteran of stints in Washington, D.C., and New York City. Texas-born Little is bearded, graying, mellow, dreamy, a painter and sculptor (a graduate of the arts program at the University of Houston) who loves to read and quote poetry. "I get a lot of my inspiration from poetry," he says. "It goes straight into the soul, works in the heart, and comes out in the garden. As a friend of mine said, 'We garden because we remember paradise.' My favorite poets are Yeats, Rilke, the sixteenth-century Persian poet Rumi, Dickinson, Wordsworth." Lewis, on the other hand, is happy reading what he calls "plane-crash novels." But they have created a brilliant working

Left: Palm fronds, banana leaves, and the vivid flowers of a golden chain tree stage a seasonal tropical riot around David Lewis's house.

Right: "We use plants as sculpture, and sculpture as plants," comments David Lewis.

relationship by melding their contrasts and pooling their passions—particularly their passion for lushly colored cast-concrete sculptures that live outdoors. The Little and Lewis partnership has irregular but well-understood boundaries: they sign all their creations with both their names, even though one of them is usually more responsible for an individual work than the other; similarly, the garden is a loose ongoing collaboration, even though they have very different approaches to plants and ideas about how to use them. Lewis, for starters, is definitely not a plantsman ("I don't get attached to plants," he confesses), and Little very definitely is and always has been ("I've been interested in plants for as long as I

remember—I get attached to the feeling plants create"). Lewis owns and lives alone in the gray-blue house at the center of the garden—he bought it in 1988 and began gardening here a couple of years later as a way of dealing with his grief over the death of his partner. Little commutes daily from his own two-and-a-half-acre woodland garden to work with Lewis in the studio/garage (equipped with full-spectrum lighting to ward off winter gloom) and in the garden. They sculpt and cast in the garden whenever the weather permits.

Travel is another area in which they collaborate—and travel in turn breathes new ideas into the garden. "We find inspiration just about everywhere we go," says Little. Mediterranean gardens and, of course, classical ruins rank high on their inspiration list: the Renaissance Villa d'Este at Tivoli, outside of Rome, with its wonderful fountains and vistas; the clipped shrubbery and magnificent sculpture of the Boboli Gardens in Florence; Gournia—a Minoan site on a hillside in Crete ("desolate," murmurs Little in recollected admiration, "the foundations and walls are mazelike"), and Lato, also in Crete ("the most beautiful site—you feel the presence of something there"). How on earth could an ancient Minoan site influence the design of a garden in a semirural suburb near Puget Sound? This would be an impossible stretch for most of us, but Little and Lewis make it look totally natural. Indeed, Lewis insists that their garden *is* an archaeological site—or at least the semblance of one, with its narrow paths between ghostly overgrown "rooms," the pitted surfaces and washed-out colors of its "masonry," its broken columns suggesting fallen grandeur. Garden as archaeological site: a unique approach that only an artist would dream up. Crazy as it sounds, it is one of the keys to the mystery of this garden. Once you look at the garden this

Left: The "rain tree" is an ingeniously crafted fountain in which water seeps through a crown of baby tears and hart's tongue fern.

Right: The gunnera leaf at the center of this foliage composition is actually cast and colored concrete. Water drips into a pool dotted with the aquatic fern *Azolla caroliniana*.

way, you begin to see why the beds are shaped and placed as they are, why the columns work so wonderfully in their varying heights and stages of "decay," how water is used.

Water. It's everywhere in this garden—pools and trickles, spouts and seeps, bowls and basins and miniature ponds—and it's amazing that Little and Lewis have incorporated so many water features on their modest one-third-acre lot without crowding or a discordant sense of competition among fountains. One of their most striking and characteristic fountains is the "rain tree"—a low, mounded, gracefully arching cast-concrete tree (imagine a cross between a mushroom and an oak) that drips water ever so gradually through a crown of baby's tears and hart's tongue ferns (Little and Lewis mixed peat moss into the concrete at the top). The rain tree stands like a great drippy stalagmite that has come half alive—or maybe it's a gnarled old dwarf whose splayed knobby "feet" rest on a cylinder of cement that rises in turn out of a circular pool studded with pots and the naked, jointed stems of *Equisetum hyemale* (horsetail—an invasive wetland pest that they keep carefully contained).

"Our passion is sculpting," remarks Lewis to the music of splashing drops. "We just happen to have a beautiful garden that the work resides in. We use plants as sculpture, and sculpture as plants." That's the second key to the Little and Lewis garden. Look around at the exuberant fronds of tropical tree ferns, the curled paddles of banana leaves, and the giant, fleshy, architectural *Gunnera* leaves; study the column capitals sprouting iris blades and ornamental grasses, the clusters of giant puffed-rice poppy buds floating over the foliage like something out of Miró, and you'll see just what Lewis means. Individual plants, even single leaves, stand out as living works of art—the swaying "stabile" of a bird-of-paradise, a frieze of water lilies—while works of art mounted on the garden walls turn out to be

Little and Lewis spent years perfecting their secret technique for casting and coloring concrete used in signature pieces like the chanterelle chair and rain tree (**left**) and the sculpture of a dove and basin (**right**).

Below: Heavenly blue containers inspired by the trumpets of morning glories contrast vibrantly with the flowers and foliage of the plants they hold.

Right: The lushness and complexity of the plantings create an aura of depth, height, and rustling tropical mystery on a third-of-an-acre lot.

painted concrete casts made from fresh-cut leaves of *Gunnera* and banana and lotus. "We use actual leaves to make our leaves, which makes them all one-of-a-kind," Little points out. "Every sculpture we do is made from concrete, and all are weatherproof." As for the color-wash technique that imbues their concrete pieces with hues that look as rich but delicately faded as old velvet, Little says its development took them years of "a great deal of trial-and-error experimentation": "As far as we know, we are the only ones doing it and it's rather a secret."

At the head of the driveway Lewis and Little have placed a gravelly skinned, terra-cotta–colored hemispheric concrete basin on a

four-foot pedestal. From a few feet back it looks rather like a pre-historic dinosaur egg that has cracked in half, and when you peer inside, you see a single floating leaf of *Macleaya cordata* reflected against the bottom curve of the egg. Plant as sculpture, sculpture as plant: by selecting and suspending this single leaf on a lens of water, these artists have transformed a rather gangly, graceless plant into something serene, almost mythical. You notice the scalloped edges of the *Macleaya* leaf and silver-felted underside as you never would if you saw the plant sprawling in a garden bed; and you can't help fingering the jagged edges of the dinosaur egg, a creation at once lumpish and strangely, ethereally fragile. The egg is one small bit of the Little and Lewis garden, but it perfectly crystallizes their wit and their aesthetic.

Lest all this sound too rarefied and mystical, it should be noted that the Little and Lewis garden is much lived in. Tables and benches and wonderfully mushroomy chairs are scattered beneath the trees for impromptu summer picnic lunches or meditative breaks from the grind of ever-mounting art commissions. The lawn is distinctly scruffy, as befits a lawn that gets walked and knelt on a lot (not in prayer but in weeding marathons, in which friends participate). Little and Lewis love warm Mediterranean climes and flee Puget Sound winters whenever they can, but during the Pacific Northwest's brief Mediterranean summer spells, they live and work in the garden and use it constantly.

"The garden grew from intuition," Little explains when asked about their garden-making process. "Basically, there was no great intellectual input—we planted things we thought we would enjoy. It developed more by going to a nursery and seeing a plant I had to have and finding space for it. I've always thought plants have a sense of their own beauty. Rilke says, 'One cannot create beauty, one can only create circumstances favorable for it.'

Left: Art or nature? After spending time in Little and Lewis's garden, you have to look twice at this massive gunnera leaf to tell if it's a concrete cast or part of a living plant.

Right: A shady corner of the garden serves as informal gallery for leaf casts.

That's a perfect axiom for the gardener. The garden is its own entity: it tells you what to do."

The garden evidently spoke especially loudly and clearly in a little corner inspired by a Roman piazza. While wandering around Rome, Little and Lewis were mesmerized by an ancient *bocca di verità*

(mouth of truth) mask spitting water into a pitted basin, and when they got home they created their own elaborately bearded interpretation, modeled on a friend's face. Their *bocca di verità* spouts water into a rectangular basin covered with a tiny-leafed floating aquatic fern *(Azolla caroliniana)*—or rather not quite covered, for the flowing water clears a perfect semicircle on the surface. The garden—or their intuition—told them to surround this delicate classical vignette with clouds of bold, splashy, large-flowered plants and vibrantly patterned foliage—a white-blooming oakleaf hydrangea; little trumpet squadrons of lemon-yellow 'Stella d'Oro' daylilies; a variegated *Ligularia*; yellow 'Sea Fire' hostas; and, swooping around overhead, a vigorous 'Nelly Moser' clematis that bursts into bloom in fluttery stripes of pink and lavender late each spring.

In the realm of color, Lewis and Little have given their combined intuition utterly free rein. One must shed any notion of a conventional Northwest palette when one enters this garden and let the eye acclimate to a wildly eclectic spectrum imported from Mexico, the American Southwest, Greece, and Provence, and distributed by the unfettered imaginations of two color-hungry artists. The haze of a purple smoke tree hovers near the pale straw stalks of a potted *Milium effusum* 'Aureum' (Bowles' golden grass); in late spring the shell-pink blooms of a venerable rhodie swarm against the blue-gray housefront like Day-Glo bumblebees, while disks of white cosmos and sprays of robin's-egg-blue forget-me-nots nod nearby. A bit later in the season the large, rectangular column-studded pool near the drive bursts into chromatically extravagant bloom: yellow nasturtiums cascade near a mass of 'Peaches and Cream' verbena; gold- and red-leafed geraniums quiver inside the trumpet of an immense heavenly blue concrete morning glory supported on a column;

Left: The bold stripes of 'Nelly Moser' clematis might overwhelm more subdued gardens but looks right at home amid Little and Lewis's tropical extravagance.

Right: The greenhouse at the back of the property is a humid tropical shrine decorated with mounds of baby tears and sprays of bougainvillea.

nearby, on the wall, a red stripe sizzles down the central vein of a blue banana leaf cast in concrete; a *Gunnera* leaf looks as purple as grape jam next to a clump of yellow grass.

And then there's the extraordinary arbor. Early on in their transformation of the property from what Lewis describes as a totally plain and naked lot with a bare lawn punctuated by a couple of rhodies and some Douglas firs, the two partners put up a row of three eight-foot-tall blue columns near the house; later they paired these columns with another three; and then one day Lewis said, "Let's take a risk and add teal-green cross members." On the Fauvist arbor that resulted, they subsequently trained the perfect plant: a rambunctious 'Paul's Himalayan Musk' rose that blooms profusely each spring in faintly blushing fragrant white flowers.

Open by appointment only, the garden attracts a steady stream of visitors who come to commission a Little and Lewis original, examine the artists' work in its "native" habitat, find inspiration for their own gardens, or simply pay homage. Lewis is always intrigued by the reactions of the people who come. "Seventy-five percent of them get it," he notes, "fifteen percent don't, and ten percent have a religious experience." It's a very odd religion—a compound of pagan and classical, sun worship and water worship, wistful nostalgia and bold innovation—and like all new visions it requires some mental and spiritual adjustment. But make no mistake: Little and Lewis are doing something new and special in their small island garden, and they are doing it in the mysterious time-honored way of artists—by instinct and passion, by luck, by ceaseless work, and by the willingness to surrender to enchantment.

The Artist's Eye

Playing with Scale: Though their lot is small, Little and Lewis have deliberately chosen plants with large, even huge, structural leaves, such as *Gunnera, Rodgersia,* and *Ligularia,* and massed them near the house or used them as focal points in beds. Similarly, they display outsized cast-concrete art objects throughout the garden—columns with exaggeratedly large capitals or shafts that are wider than they are "supposed" to be relative to their height. An impossibly tall column rises next to one that has been truncated; a garden chair in the shape of an enormous soft golden-orange morel mushroom looms like a curved fungal throne, with fluted spines up its base and along its back. The effect of these distortions and juxtapositions is to intrigue and amuse by throwing us off balance—rather like a surrealistic canvas by Dalí or a collage by Max Ernst. As Little puts it, "Little crowded beds with oversized plants make people feel childlike." In this garden, it's impossible to resist the temptation to wander down fuzzy paths, peer around corners, follow the sound of water across bridges that span tiny rivers. There's a festive, Fellini-esque quality to this garden, a feeling of having stepped into a wonderfully alien world and being enveloped by pleasingly grotesque shapes and textures. Little and Lewis accomplish this quite deftly by playing with scale in subtle and fantastic ways.

New Twists with Containers: Little and Lewis love containers, but they eschew the current fashion of cramming pots with miniature jungles of intertwining plants in harmonious colors and textures. "We just do lovely specimen plants," says Little. "One plant to a pot. It's much calmer and less flashy." It also allows the individual plant to reach perfection of form and culture. For the most part they limit themselves to fairly standard terra-cotta pots, along with their own handmade concrete containers. But though the pots themselves are simple and straightforward, considerable artistry has been lavished on the massing, grouping, and arranging of the containers. On the patio near their front door Little and Lewis have created a marvelous container tableau of a very large bird-of-paradise plant *(Caesalpinia gilliesii), Acidanthera bicolor, Epiphyllum* (a tropical orchid cactus), *Ensete ventricosum* (which looks like a banana tree, with 10- to 20-foot-long leaves), and various types of bromelaids. The plants, extraordinarily lush and healthy, are placed so that they complement and comment on each other perfectly. You notice each plant in each pot: the shape and texture of the leaves; the shadows the plant and its container cast; the play of color. Little and Lewis use columns to elevate and highlight individual plants and to lend scale and variety to the groupings of containers. The overall effect is a living composition—a kind of large-scale mosaic in which each piece is as important as the whole.

Fearless, Unconventional Use of Color: Little and Lewis often spend winters in a little town in central Mexico, and they freely use the bold, bright colors of the desert to accent the lush green foliage of their garden. Wolflike masks painted in saturated shades of turquoise, orange, violet, hot pink, and terra-cotta grace the garden's thickly textured sculptural leaves, fountains, and frescoes. Foliage and flowers are equally riotous. A bright blue bench draws the eye to a bridge inset with pink medallions, with a cobalt jug beyond it. These are not the pastels that Northwest gardeners inherited from their British gardening forebears and have grown accustomed to using under soft gray skies; rather, they are the antithesis of gray, and they spark and enhance all the greenness of the Northwest environment

Making the Most of a Small, Shady Corner: Between the rear of the house and the greenhouse is a shady, rather cramped passage that many gardeners would have chosen to ignore or neglect. But Little and Lewis have worked wonders here by employing cool colors and a limited plant palette—in strong contrast to the rest of the property. They have hidden the house foundation behind a row of deeply veined blue-leafed *Hosta sieboldiana* fringed with a groundcover of oxalis; staghorn ferns and a climbing hydrangea decorate the back wall of the house and tie in nicely with the color and texture of the hostas; and off to the side stands a stately black elderberry *(Sambucus nigra).* Harmony and restraint are the main notes here—a relief from (and an interesting comment on) the rest of the property, and a soothing transition into the hushed, humid, dappled greenhouse.

Far left: Painters Grant Leier and Nixie Barton mix weird yard-sale objects with plants in their garden on Vancouver Island.

Left: A bird house tarted up with fake fruit and wrought iron finials.

Brave Gardeners of the Funky Baroque:
Grant Leier and Nixie Barton

"I was so tired of seeing gardens where everything is raw and natural," muses Grant Leier as he sits looking out at a garden from which "raw" and "natural" have been banished like noxious weeds. "That's why our garden uses so much glass and metal and plastic—I love plastic. Nixie and I wanted to decorate our garden with stuff we designed. We wanted to introduce things that shouldn't be there —really unexpected elements. If you have driftwood, you should at least paint it bright orange to tart

it up a bit. A garden without manipulation is really dull."

"Dull" is the last word anyone would use to describe the three-quarter-acre garden on a nine-acre lot that painters Grant Leier and Nixie Barton have created around their house, studio, and gallery on a rural back road outside of Nanaimo on the east side of Vancouver Island. Working together with enviable accord and unfailing good humor, this husband-and-wife team has transformed a former pasture on a hobby farm—a flat, white-rail-fenced grassy expanse punctuated by a couple of trees—into a kind of explosion of art, plants, found objects, gates, candelabra, posts, tiles, marbles, water features, shrines, chairs, containers, and, yes, lots of plastic. The land's flatness remains, as do the trees; but everything has been filled in, colored over, built up, reoriented, and framed with a series of highly original makeshift fences. If you erase everything Nixie and Grant have added, you can still make out the original relationships between house, shed-turned-studio, and barn-turned-gallery: each building sits a stone's throw apart from the others, more or less plunked down for convenience in the flat expanse, the gallery set back deeper into the property than the studio, and the studio deeper than the house. Deeper still, at the end of an ungardened field, the woods begin. But Barton and Leier have put in so many beds, borders, arches, eddies, paths, objects, pots, columns, nooks and crannies between and around the buildings that an innocent stroll becomes a circuitously disorienting voyage of discovery—a remarkable feat given the fact that the cultivated part of the yard is less than an acre. It's a garden so full, busy, happy, and humming that it beggars description: no matter how many superlatives one rolls out, the garden always tops them. The Barton/Leier garden is like a carnival without the tawdriness; it's gothic with levity; funky Baroque; New Orleans luxe with breezy northern clarity; folk-art primitive crossed

Left: A twig chair, clearly not meant to be sat on, takes its place alongside irises as a decorative element in this fence planting.

Right: It's hard to find an unadorned surface in Barton and Leier's exuberant outdoor space.

with high Bohemian splendor. If Gauguin had had a sense of humor and a green thumb and had been married to someone like *New Yorker* cartoonist Roz Chast, this is the kind of garden they would have created on Tahiti—if only plastic had been invented.

Barton and Leier—both in their early forties, both blond and on the tall side, she with a wonderful swept-back mane and startled-looking blue eyes, he with soft features and retro black glasses, both warm and loose and quick to laugh—create dazzling, crowded, hot-colored, preternaturally lively acrylic paintings. Painters first; gardeners second—but painters and gardeners in very much the same style. Never do they set up an easel in their garden, or even bring branches or flowers into the studio—but in a way their artwork is the canvas-and-acrylic equivalent of their brimming beds and borders. The art and the garden have a common spirit: the impulse to fill every square inch with something hot, bright, and wonderful; to decorate until surfaces sing; to include, amass, accumulate, and display. In one of Leier's paintings, a portrait of a dog is placed squarely on top of a portrait of a spray of red rhodies, both portraits framed individually in images of leaves, fruits, and flowers, and then framed together in red and yellow scrollwork, and then framed yet again in a painted quilt of hearts, patches, and more leaves. A painted message above and below the dog reads: "Count Your Blessings & Celebrate Often." Count, bless, celebrate often are the guiding principles of the garden too: don't omit anything good, lest you miss a chance for one more joyous occasion.

It's clear, when you question Barton and Leier closely about their process of art and garden-making, that they haven't put a lot of thought into how they collaborate or where they draw the line between them. They just do it. As Barton says, "We garden the same way we paint: we just start. No sketch, no plans."

Left: Who cares what the birds think? This artistically retouched birdbath, one of many in the garden, looks great against a halo of late spring flowers.

Right: Nixie Barton and Grant Leier collaborate on their garden and paint side by side in the studio behind them.

Their painting styles, when you first see a wall of their pictures hung together in the old barn they have ingeniously transformed into a gallery, look very similar—but on closer inspection one quickly learns to distinguish a Barton from a Leier. It comes as no surprise to learn that they have never painted together on the same canvas, though they share a studio and work side by side (or used to before their son Grayson was born five and a half years ago; now they tend to work in shifts). Barton's art, though it has a common palette with Leier's (violet, cobalt blue, cadmium yellow, quinacridone red), is softer, looser, earthier, more sensuous, more romantic, less ironic. ("I adore Matisse," says Barton, "for me he is number one." Leier lists David Hockney and Andy Warhol as his heroes.) Barton tends to paint still lifes of fruits, flowers, plates, vases and the occasional animal, while Leier juggles images of dogs, cats, people, and restaurant interiors with organic forms of plants and abstract plantlike shapes. Perhaps it would be fair to say that they work in the same school—like Giorgione and Titian or Bonnard and Vuillard.

In the garden, on the other hand, the collaboration is complete—and completely unpremeditated. As Leier explains, when they bought the property in 1994, they jumped in together head first ("ass backwards," is actually how he described it) and started gardening pretty much from day one, digging beds where they felt a bed should be, laying paths, erecting pergolas and fences, "going crazy with this amount of space." But always together. They'd hit the local nurseries, return with scads of must-have plants, and start throwing them into the ground without even bothering to amend the soil (a move they now regret and are working hard to correct). Leier went through a major ivy phase, and Barton admits to getting a bit exasperated when yet another tray of ivy

Left: Barton and Leier layer plants, objects, and structures like fences and gates to create dense, rhythmic garden vignettes.

Right: This central pergola, one of the garden's first structures, took shape around four stately white columns that Leier picked up on the cheap.

seedlings appeared ("If Grant sees something he likes, he buys fifty of them"). Barton tends to go through color periods—her blue period, her white period. Currently she's in her black period, and everywhere you look there are silky, glossy, mysterious-looking black leaves and flowers popping out of the ground: their little greenhouse is chockablock with black poppy seedlings, grown from seeds painstakingly collected last year from a single seed head; a handsome glazed tub sprouts a halo of black mondo grass interspersed with black clover; in another container the first tender shoots of black Alberta wheat are just starting to emerge. Somewhere, Barton claims, there is a black tree peony scheduled to bloom. Though black is Barton's current thing, Leier is an enthusiastic comrade in arms. There are no "his" and "hers" patches of this garden, and rarely ever squabbles over style or content.

Born in Vancouver, raised in Victoria, and educated at the University of Victoria and Malaspina College in Nanaimo, Barton met Leier in 1983 in Victoria, where both of them were living and painting and active in the gallery scene. Leier himself had migrated to Victoria via Lloydminster, Alberta, where he was born and raised, Alberta College of Art in Calgary, where he was educated, and the Illustrator's Workshop in New York City, where he picked up valuable experience that he has used in his flourishing career as a commercial illustrator (which he still pursues side by side with his painting for gallery shows).

When they moved out to this residential country road, their reaction to having so much space all around them was, as Barton puts it, "Oh my God, where to start?" Being artists and the kinds of people they are, they naturally started by erecting an elaborate pergola right smack in the middle of the yard. Leier acquired four stately white columns that look like something off the set of the Taylor/Burton *Cleopatra*

Left: Peeling white columns, plaster cherubs, and wisteria give the pergola a louche, New Orleans aura.

Right: Gaudily painted animals and figures cut out of sheet metal crop up all over the garden.

movie, and the pergola grew from there. "We naively planted four wisterias—blue and white—one next to each column," recalls Leier, staring up at the dense thicket of intertwining stems that has resulted, "and we couldn't bear to prune anything." Actually, the storm of wisteria foliage is probably the most subdued thing about this pergola: over the years, they have decorated wildly, carving birds into the crosspieces, setting a dramatic birdbath dead center, planting drifts of primroses in the surrounding beds, introducing

Below: Statues representing the arts of painting, music, architecture, and sculpture preside over a sunny corner of the garden.

Right: Just about anything that can stand up to foot traffic gets cemented into the collage-like garden paths – plastic toys, marbles, glass blocks, horse shoes.

a plastic bulldog on a plant stand, hanging a rococo chandelier from the rafters, putting in a menagerie of statues in various media, so now the pergola has been transmogrified from *Cleopatra* to Fellini's *Satyricon.*

Another early project was to lay down a path linking their circa 1970 army-issue house (actually two army houses that got knit together) with the shed-turned-studio. Barton lined the path with a lavender hedge and planted "every *Euphorbia* in the world," and the garden was off and running. At some point they transformed the front of the studio itself, dressing up the façade with masks, birdhouses and birdcages, ceramic images of the Virgin of Guadalupe, blue candles, carvings, and a Georgia O'Keeffe bull's

skull, and massing pots of grasses and sedum in the little patio in front. Inside, four of Leier's vibrant, pattern-rich paintings in various stages of progress hang side by side ("I always have four going at once," he explains). The wall opposite is lined with shelves packed to overflowing with the gleanings of hundreds of flea markets, garage sales, and swap meets: masks and lamps, trolls and figurines, Indonesian puppets, kitschy little doodads from every cheesy decade of the last century. "It's exciting to find items of questionable taste," comments Leier, "put them into new situations, and significantly elevate their status." Such questionable-taste objects gain status simply by being noticed—but the status boost reaches new heights when Leier and Barton incorporate them into their art or their garden or both. Some artists keep sketchbooks or scrapbooks: Leier and Barton keep this shrine of evocative objects.

In Barton's fond, bemused description, their approach to garden design sounds like controlled (or rampant) chaos: "We design as we go—we just go nuts to fill the property up—basically winging it." But if you spend enough time here studying the arrangement of plants and objects, you will eventually detect some organizing themes and principles. Yes, the garden is free-form and exuberantly decorated, but as with their paintings, beneath the vibrant surface there's an underlying structure built of parallel forms, interlocking planes, and emphatic outlines. Clumps of the same species are repeated at intervals in a bed to set up rhythms; stones, logs, pots, and other rounded shapes define beds and borders; gates and pergolas add a kind of skyline that lends scale to the beds and provides an upper story for climbers.

Take the vegetable garden, tucked away between the back of the studio and the entrance to the gallery. Two grand, freestanding porticoes face each other on opposite sides of the generous square. These stunning structures (made from pieces of the old roof they had pulled off their studio), bedecked with birdhouses, plastic fruit, and dried flowers, look like the gates to some hippie king's private estate. In fact they usher you into a collection of raised beds overflowing with the oddest array of edible plants you've ever

laid eyes on—Egyptian walking onions whose tops flop over and root themselves into new plants; Japanese celery that blooms in January and sends up huge umbrella-like leaves that faint on hot summer days, only to revive in the cool of evening; gorgeous thickets of leeks; gnarled, sculptural asparagus (gnarled because, as it turns out, Leier and Barton don't really eat their vegetables—they grow them because they like the way they look).

There's something else very cool going on here. Barton and Leier have turned on its head the ordinary garden relationship between plants and things. In most of our gardens, objects are second-class citizens that crouch demurely next to the plants and wait to be noticed as backdrop, punctuation, or visual relief. But in Barton and Leier's vegetable garden, around their pond, and under and over their pergolas, objects and plants hold the same rank and serve the same purpose. On an outside wall of their studio is a wonderful vignette: a shell-pink camellia and a white-flowering climbing hydrangea have been trained to grow up against the cadmium-yellow wood siding; at intervals in the vigorous branches of these happy plants, Leier has fixed his collection of plastic figurines of wrestlers and alligators. Who's tougher—a rampant vine or a testosterone-pumped wrestler? The point is, plants and things embrace (or compete) as equals here: they coexist on a continuum that ranges from pure beauty to pure trashiness. There are plants for the sake of plants and objects for the sake of objects here—all mixed up and placed with an unerring sense of humor and rightness.

Which is not to say that the plants are treated shabbily or irreverently. Barton in particular has her favorites and she coddles them along to lush, crisp perfection like any horticultural fanatic: foxtail lilies, big, floppy-leafed *Ligularia*, *Dracunculus vulgaris* (a delightfully rude and gangling member of the skunk cabbage family), the Australian bottlebrush plant (a tender shrub with brushy flowers that they winter over in the greenhouse), broom (not the dreadful duckling-yellow kind that is taking over our empty lots, but well-mannered broom in soft buttery or plush russet shades), *Gunnera,* and society garlic (which bears airy, starry, purple flowers) are Barton's reigning pets. There are plant beds arranged by color—though obviously not quite as chromatically pristine as Vita Sackville-West's "white garden"—and others laid out to accommodate members of the same family or zone. Leier is particularly proud of his tropical corner, planted with three kinds of ginger, a hardy banana tree, blue poppies (not, strictly speaking, tropical, but exotic looking), and wine-colored peonies. But no bed or patch or border in this garden, no matter how thick with plants, is devoid of decoration or out of sight of some sort of human-made structure or object. The result is that the plants become part of a larger, more intricate, more resonant composition than is possible in the conventional plant-centered bed—a multimedia composition in which kitsch and horticulture, pop art and schlock art, flea-market chic and botanical haute couture play off each other, chiming in and fading out as you wander around.

The funky archipelago that Grant Leier and Nixie Barton have raised in the pleasant backwater between their house and gallery is one more wonderful sign that a garden can be so much more than well-grown plants. To break out of the mold of the conventional plant-centered garden, you just need wit, courage, humor, a healthy appreciation for the sublime and the ridiculous, a knack for arranging things in space and time, an instinct for form and color, an eye for neat stuff, and an openness to odd combinations and novel twists of fate. In short, you need to be an artist.

Right: A vigorous spray of lupine and a chicken-on-a-stick by the garden pool.

The Artist's Eye

Recycle, Reuse, Reveal: Barton and Leier are great collectors of "stuff" from flea markets and garage sales, and their garden brims with all sorts of weird, recycled found objects. Big spherical stone rollers used for commercial fishing nets (they look like King Kong's bowling balls) become decorative garden globes or convenient "vases" for "dream sticks" (wrought-iron stakes capped with finials and fitted with little wire cages that hold Chinese glass balls). Old packing crates frame a charming little garden patch that Leier has created around a former duck pond. Extra roofing material goes into the elaborate gates that stand guard over the vegetable garden. Perhaps the triumph of their recycling projects is the fence that runs along the front of the property between gallery and house: Leier and Barton asked the local metalworking shop to save the sheets of metal out of which their folk-art animals are stamped, and they turned these used sheets into fence panels. At first glance, they resemble metallic Swiss cheese punched out in abstract patterns; but if you take a closer look, you realize that the cutouts are actually animal shapes—chickens, gulls, moose, running dogs—with a different animal on each panel. The fence has a weird M. C. Escher aura about it.

Amazing Paths and Pavers: Leier and Barton began paving their garden paths with cement but quickly moved on to more inspired, even bizarre materials. Rocks and bits of broken mirror are embedded in the thick concrete underneath the pergola that stands outside their gallery; the vegetable-garden paths are a collage of glass blocks, old brick, tile samples, plastic fish, marbles, and stone "health balls" from China. Pretty much anything that can be cemented down and walked on gets tossed in. Some of their first efforts have begun to buckle and heave over time, but Leier and Barton have gotten more professional in their approach to zany paving, and their latest efforts, while still funky, are tight and permanent.

Structure for the Sake of Structure: Why does a garden gate have to lead anywhere? Why does a post have to hold something up? Why does a chair have to be sat on? We put plants in our gardens simply because we like the way they look, smell, or combine with what's already there—so why not take the same approach with objects? "I like the look of chairs," Leier remarks when questioned about the abundance of seating in his garden. "I stick broken ones into beds. I just like the way it looks." Tall posts painted in crayon colors have sprouted up all over the place; in the future they may hold baskets of drought-tolerant flowers, but for now they simply preside over the islands of plants like lampposts without lamps. Near the vegetable patch, two of these posts have been joined with a cross member, painted red, and capped with fancy black wrought-iron scrollwork to create a freestanding gate to nowhere in particular. Two flourishing red Japanese maples flank the gate, and nearby there is a large four-story birdhouse—more like a bird condo—with a red roof and blue and yellow walls. The proliferation of structure in this section of the garden creates the occasion, and the plants follow. Similarly, posts and columns elsewhere in the garden provide ready excuses for putting in new vines: Virginia creeper, potato vine, clematis, and silver lace vine (Polygonum aubertii), a "never-fail" climber that bears clusters of white airy flowers in late summer.

Go Crazy: "Be the Brave Gardener" advises a sign at the entrance to the outdoor gallery space where Leier and Barton sell the dream sticks, animals on stakes, candelabra, and plant stands that they fashion out of sheet metal and wrought iron. Leier and Barton epitomize garden bravery: never afraid to take risks, break rules, and be crazy, they have filled their garden with unexpected images, objects, and combinations. Wax tapers in the garden? Wouldn't they sag in the sun? That only makes them look more interesting. Plastic frogs swarm all over a birdhouse. A metal moose cutout peeks out from behind four adorable concrete statues of cherubs representing the four arts of painting, music, architecture, and sculpture. So many of us take an overly solemn approach to gardening, pondering the placement of each seedling as if the fate of the republic depended on it. Leier and Barton prefer to jump right in "ass backwards," mix it up, have fun, and go crazy.

Far left: European hornbeams trained into gothic "windows" form a backdrop for bread seed poppies (*Papaver somniferum*), interplanted with *Allium* 'Globemaster' and bronze fennel.

Left: An *Angelica*, its maroon flower stalk just beginning to unfurl, is set off by a sea of yellow *Lysimachia nummularia* 'Aurea'.

10

The Science of Artistry, the Artistry of Science:
Dan Hinkley's Heronswood

Plant lust is a recognized condition (some might say malady) of gardeners. We suffer from a near-desperate desire to be first with the newest, the best, the hottest plant. But Dan Hinkley is always, always first—not only does he have the best plants before anyone else can get their hands on them, but he grows plants that most gardeners have not yet heard of. This is because Hinkley has been off climbing the mountains of Nepal, searching the valleys of Tasmania, collecting seed from plants not yet

cultivated to bring back to his five-acre home and nursery on the Kitsap Peninsula in Washington State. In a year or two, gardeners around the globe will be clamoring for the plants that now flourish here. Hinkley's personal garden reveals that before he was a plant collector, and before he was the founder (along with partner Robert Jones) of a fabulously successful mail-order business in rare and unusual plants, he was a gardener first and foremost. And he still is. Hinkley has taken his excitement at seeing plants growing in their native habitats on his treks about the globe, and used that sense of wonder, and his unique horticultural knowledge, to create a sensuous, magical garden that's almost childlike in its exuberance.

Hinkley is truly an artist—one who uses plants as his medium of expression. While other artists use clay, paint, or molten glass as their primary artistic medium, Hinkley uses dirt, flowers, and leaves as the stuff of artistic expression. He deals with the same problems as all artists—how to use color and form as well as concepts of volume and space to shape raw materials into fine art. And serious gardeners will tell you that creating gardens may well be the most difficult of all the arts.

Garden historian Mac Griswold has described gardening as the slowest of the performing arts, but the patience it requires is only one of its challenges. A vast array of plants (all with binomial or trinomial Latin names, which, once mastered by the gardener, are inevitably changed by taxonomists); the vagaries of weather; colors that shift with sun, shade, and length of bloom; plant growth; and seasonal change are just a few of the formidable obstacles. Thousands of trees, shrubs, perennials, annuals, bulbs, and vines each have their own natures, habits, hardiness, and methods of propagation, all of which the gardener must study to grow them successfully. Hinkley's approach to garden-making is as gallant and

Left: *Rosa* 'Eddie's Jewel' cascades over a planting of conifers, perennials, and ornamental grasses.

Right: An oversize pot bursting with a bronze phormium interlaced with the yellow leaves and pink blooms of *Spirea japonica* 'Magic Carpet'.

perhaps as foolhardy as that of an artist who paints huge canvases in pure gold leaf, or makes mosaics out of diamonds and rubies. He uses rare and unusual plants, which he has personally gathered from around the globe, as the raw material for his art.

No one alive today personifies the art of gardening more than Dan Hinkley. It is neither Hinkley's encyclopedic knowledge of plants nor his willingness to travel the earth to find new ones that has earned him a lengthy and admiring profile in *The New York Times* Sunday magazine and regular appearances on Martha Stewart's television show. This is unprecedented celebrity for a gardener, and it has happened because Hinkley knows how to arrange plants with show-stopping originality and beauty as well as how to grow them perfectly. In short, it is Hinkley's artistry with plants that continues to astound and beguile gardeners from around the world, turning Heronswood into a mecca for garden enthusiasts. A visit to Heronswood is akin to a religious pilgrimage for garden lovers: Hinkley's private garden is the holy of holies of our current cult of rare and unusual plants.

As you tour the gardens, it becomes clear that Hinkley has created a plant encyclopedia of a garden that expresses his sense of awe at the proliferation of plants. These five acres, which include 9,000 flourishing taxa, look like nothing else you've ever seen— you just keep gasping at one ravishing thing after another. Hinkley himself isn't much help in defining his artistry: he is too busy doing it, talking about it, writing about it. "The English are my inspiration—not the English border but their sense of plants- manship, of growing plants to perfection." Somehow, Hinkley has taken this incredible respect for each plant, added his knowledge of the conditions under which it grows in the wild, considered all the

Left: A cloud of white-flowered *Crambe cordifolia* towers over the magenta-flowered, yellow-leaved *Geranium* 'Ann Folkard', ruby *Astrantia major* 'Hadspen Blood', and the long-blooming maroon buttons of *Knautia macedonica*.

Right: Frilly bracts of the sea holly *Eryngium alpinum* shown off by the yellow foliage of *Spirea japonica* 'Magic Carpet'.

aspects of his site, and put it all together to create a garden unlike any other ever made.

Unless you were as astute about plants as Hinkley himself—and who among us is?—you might not guess that this garden is both laboratory and showcase for the plants he brings back from Japan, Sikkim, Korea, China, Tasmania, Nepal, Vietnam, Mexico, and Chile. Specimens are not lined up for examination, nor does the garden consist of tiny eccentricities that you need a magnifying glass to appreciate. Rather it is an explosion of colorful, lusty plants, mingling and spreading about. So often, plant collecting itself is the consuming passion, and though that is true with Hinkley, he has a vision beyond collecting, and understands that garden-making is much more than horticulture. It is in the intimate garden spaces surrounding his home that Hinkley grows the plants from the seed he collects. Tiny treasures like the variegated *Hacquetia epipactus* that Hinkley brought back, not from a mountainous trek to China but from the garden of a friend in Surrey, England, is the no-one-else-has-it-yet kind of plant that most collectors would carefully coddle. In Hinkley's garden it is simply one remarkable plant among a great many others, set out into the garden to rub shoulders with its less distinguished relatives, arranged so that its double hit of variegation (flowers and leaves both edged in cream so cunningly as to appear that someone painted it just so) blends in with the overall picture. Instead of falling into the trap of the botanist, who, in the words of famed British horticulturist Wilfred Blunt, "wants to grow what he can't and preferably where it won't," Hinkley uses his vast knowledge of plants to grow each plant so ideally that it reaches the height of its own possible perfection.

Hinkley certainly looks like a gardener—he is big, burly, bearded, balding, often smudged with soil—but he doesn't quite fit one's image of a what a garden celebrity looks like, whatever that is. Maybe it's just that he's so modest, funny, self-deprecating. One of his greatest charms is his effectiveness at bringing new gardeners into the fold by sharing tales of mistakes as well as triumphs. In his book *The Explorer's Garden: Rare and Unusual Perennials* (Timber Press, 1999) he tells the story of one rescuing a Japanese anemone that had been tossed onto a compost heap, riding home on his bike with the plant tucked proudly under his arm. How comforting to know that this man, renowned around the world for his knowledge of plants, once thought Japanese anemones to be choice.

Hinkley, who grew up in Michigan, developed a love of plants early. By the age of four

Left: A bonsai pine tree rests amid the tawny blades of *Carex comans*.

Right: A Grecian "ruin" made by artists George Little and David Lewis is one of the surprises to be found along the paths of Heronswood's 2.5-acre woodland garden.

he was already collecting moss to grow on his windowsill in one of those blue Dairy Queen banana split containers. A feisty neighbor named Mrs. Newman taught him to tap sugar maples and make maple sugar candy. Years later, he wrote his thesis on the maples in Seattle's Washington Park Arboretum in pursuit of his master's degree in horticulture from the University of Washington.

The Heronswood catalogue lists 2,700 different plants for sale, each described in Hinkley's humorous, enthusiastic prose. *The New York Times* calls the catalogue "a major literary artifact in the world of gardening ephemera." It probably represents the most comprehensive array of unusual trees, shrubs, vines, and perennials offered by any nursery in America. When asked why he continues to search the globe for new plants, when he already offers for sale ten times more than most of us could ever dream of growing, Hinkley answers with more questions: "How many plants are enough? The simple answer is that we, as keen gardeners, will always want to experiment with new things. Aren't there already plenty of fabrics and colors of paint and enough automobile designs to last us forever?"

Hinkley's genuine fondness for the plants and his continuing wonder at their various charms pour out in every word he utters. In a walk through his woodland garden, Hinkley rhapsodizes about a cobra lily *(Arisaema nepenthoides)* he discovered on a mountaintop in Nepal. "Look at the spathe on that flower—it must be three feet long. Have you ever seen anything like this?" Yes, indeed, this cobra lily is amazing—but so are scores and scores of other plants all around it. A plant for which Heronswood is famous, *Corydalis flexuosa* 'Blue Panda', grows in thick colonies of ferny foliage with electric blue flowers held aloft from spring through fall. On every day of the year, some variety of blue corydalis is in bloom somewhere in Heronswood's gardens. In summer, a lily relative so magnificent in both size and fragrance as to invite disbelief, towers to fifteen feet in the woodland: *Cardiocrinum giganteum* var. *giganteum* takes seven

Dan Hinkley, with Springer Spaniel Collé, and Robert Jones, left, in a rare moment of repose.

years to bloom, and when it does its ten-inch-long drooping bells waft astoundingly sweet perfume through the garden.

Hinkley and Jones began the garden in the autumn of 1987, when they moved into the little rambler across Puget Sound from metropolitan Seattle. The property consisted of four horse paddocks, a line of rhododendrons planted beneath the eaves of the house, and a silver maple in the backyard. The woodland was a dense tangle of elderberry, nettles, and bracken fern. As they cleared, they discovered old moss-laden stumps, which they left as a reminder of the woodland's age, and also as an opportunity to copy nature by planting the stumps with red huckleberries *(Vaccinium parvifolium)*. Today, the 2.5-acre sloping woodland garden leads from road to house, an enchanted and wondrous place, etched with a network of sunken trails, one of which leads to what appears to be a Grecian ruin. Made by artists George Little and David Lewis, this temple of drippy columns and elephantine *Petasites japonicus* leaves echoes the enormity and primeval nature of the *Gunneras* that thrive beneath the trees in the wetlands. This overscale remnant, half-submerged in water and leaves to give the illusion of antiquity, emphasizes the primeval nature of the woodland. *Rosa mulliganii* twines up a western red cedar *(Thuja plicata)*. Beneath the trees, bordering the meandering paths, are the most exotic and painstakingly gathered of Hinkley's collections: cyclamen, *Arisaema*, *Polygonatum*, maples, hydrangeas, corydalis, and *Erythronium*.

The transition from woodland to the gardens around the house brings a startling change of atmosphere, as you emerge from the shaded density of the woodland to a burst of sun, color, and crisp design. The massive perennial borders are laced with a backbone of deciduous shrubs chosen for outstanding foliage, enclosed by a hedge of *Thuja occidentalis* 'Holmstrup'. Favorite shrubs here include *Deutzia setchuenensis* var. *corymbiflora*, *Berberis vulgaris* 'Royal Cloak', and *Philadelphus coronarius* 'Variegatus'. No, you won't find any of these plants in your neighborhood nursery, but like so many other plants at Heronswood they look so tantalizingly familiar that you can almost guess what they are—the *Philadelphus* is a cream-splashed

variation of the familiar mock-orange, the 'Royal Cloak' a particularly deep purple barberry. Old-fashioned, new-fashioned, rare, common—it doesn't matter; each plant is used to its best effect, part of the overall canvas, and is placed where it will receive the conditions it needs to grow into its best possible form. The artistry of science, the science of artistry.

The house is surrounded by a series of intimate gardens, thickly planted yet clearly divided by stone walkways and curves of lawn. Two small ornamental pools add to the geometry, accented by the spectacular 150-foot curve of arbor that embraces the back of the garden. This colonnade serves as support for an intertwining medley of vines, their tendrils and flowers mixing together to form a tapestry of foliage and bloom throughout the year. The arbor was designed by Jones and planted by Hinkley. "Robert thinks spatially, I think botanically. I simply move in when he is finished, and plant it," Hinkley explains.

The "blue border" alongside the lawn is a long sweep of yellows and blues, planted to brighten the gloom of cloudy Northwest skies. Hardy agapanthus, cultivars of *Iris siberica*, and *Buddleia fallowiana* 'Lochinch' all provide the reflection of the wished-for cloudless blue sky, while puddles of chartreuse creeping jenny (*Lysimachia nummularia* 'Aurea') and bright yellow fluffs of *Hakonechloa macra* 'Aureola' provide a rhythmic (if illusory) reflection of warm sunshine. Despite this obvious color mastery, Hinkley says, "I am unlearning the importance of color in the garden, unless it comes from foliage. Size, texture, scale, and contrast are the most important." The front borders rely on both woody and herbaceous plants for all seasons of the year (the Michigan boy in Hinkley delights in all the possibilities of winter gardening). *Aralia elata* 'Variegata' spreads its cream-splashed branches outside the breakfast nook window, a pair of

Left: Layers of foliage and flower—poppies, bronze fennel, and the taller purple balls of *Allium* 'Globemaster'—create a textural composition.

Right: Heronswood Nursery, a mecca for gardeners, features rare and unusual plants gathered from around the globe.

Sorbus forrestii provide autumn color and whitish-pink fruits, and two evergreen viburnums (*V. propinquum* and *V. cinnamomifolium*) lend winter presence.

You would expect such an ambitious garden as Heronswood, the home garden of a horticulturist and an architect, to be perfectly planned, endlessly drawn. Hinkley describes the process quite differently, as one of nearly organic, intuitive growth, with plenty of room for inspiration and aberration. "The garden began in numerous pockets that ultimately grew together and became one," he says. "Planting directly around the house came first, but on the first weekend, when we still had boxes to unpack, I took out my frustration by planting a hedge. I would now reconsider planting anything in the garden when you are mad. The emotions remain attached to it as it grows."

Clearly, most of the emotions that have gone into this garden are happy and intensely creative, but an emotional, complicated garden it remains. It's multilayered, both with plants and with memories, for in his garden Hinkley celebrates the many friends who have shared their plants and their knowledge. He describes it all more simply: "My garden is not meant as a showpiece. It is classroom and altar, prompting a genuine appreciation for plants." Here Hinkley worships his plants with great affection and admiration, at the same time evaluating each mercilessly as to its gardenworthiness. If gardens could be said to be the mirror of the mind, then Dan Hinkley's garden reveals a mind of tireless complexity and innovation, capable of translating the science of horticulture into gardens of great artistry. It is also said that gardens are an expression of a gardener's passage through the world. If so, Hinkley is leaving an awfully large and impressive footprint. But let's let him have the last word: "Don't spend too much time analyzing it—it is just a bunch of wonderful plants jammed in together."

The Artist's Eye

Plants as Structure: Most of the structure in the Heronswood gardens is created by the artful choice and placement of the plants themselves. Perennial borders are enclosed not by walls or fences but by a living green hedge of *Thuja occidentalis* 'Holmstrup'. Almost every tree or shrub serves as scaffold for a vine, and a newer garden to the west of the house is divided into two rooms by a hedging of *Carpinus betulus* 'Fastigiata' (European hornbeam) pruned to create the effect of gothic windows. This living screen creates an undulating rhythm of transparency and solidity that could not be achieved by a structure built of wood, metal, or brick. "Anything that doesn't migrate south for the winter becomes structure in the garden," explains Hinkley. "A simply good plant, well grown and maintained, probably cannot be surpassed in effect by any artificial structure." Spoken like an artist who uses plants as his medium.

Punctuation: No matter how spectacular and unusual the plants in the borders, they don't have to carry the show by themselves—Hinkley never passes up the chance for an exclamation mark. A square bed of black mondo grass (*Ophiopogon planiscapus* 'Nigrescens') in the middle of a paved path has a narrow *Taxus baccata* 'Beanpole' tree rising up out of its center, a mirror image of the shape made by the fountain in the arbor directly across from it. For a hit of exoticism, oversized pots are planted with the fleshy blue leaves of agaves, or with spiky phormium laced with thorny purple barberry for a punch of color and texture. At the point where the axes of the gravel paths cross, a huge pot sits dead center, in which a bronze phormium holds a froth of yellow-leafed, pink-flowered *Spirea japonica* 'Magic Carpet' in its generous arms.

Historical (and Prehistoric) Reference: Although Hinkley and Jones have worked for years to transform a Douglas fir woodland into a nursery and ornamental gardens, there are plenty of references to the property's real and mythic past. The bog garden is rimmed about by the remains of large tree stumps, along with *Gunnera* leaves so huge as to suggest a dinosaur's dinner plate. Heronswood is a finely tuned and groomed garden, but sections of the woodland and the bog garden remain naturalistic enough to remind the visitor of the primeval majesty of the Northwest woods. The sheer size of the woodland garden (2.5 acres) and the ancient history suggested by the size of its trees are played upon by a sunken Grecian ruin, suggesting the remnants of an earlier civilization.

Room to Romp: Gardeners commonly start out growing annuals and then progress through flowering perennials, foliage plants, and eventually to vines—so it's no surprise that vines are a passion of a highly evolved gardener like Hinkley. The problem with vines, as every gardener realizes at some point, is that most are amazingly aggressive and need more space than you ever imagined. To solve this problem while providing a backdrop to the garden, Robert Jones designed a sturdy 150-foot curved arbor that supports dozens of different vines that intermingle in pleasing patterns of foliage and overlaps of bloom. Here honeysuckle mixes with a purple potato vine (*Solanum crispum* 'Glasnevin'), various akebias, variegated kiwi (*Actinidia kolomikta*) with splashes of cream and watermelon on its green leaves, and dozens of clematis.

Color Association: When you have, literally, thousands and thousands of different plants to play with in your own garden, how do you arrange them? One method that has proved successful for Hinkley is color segregation, as in the stunning blue and yellow border. In the four quadrants of the perennial borders, color schemes range from near white to deep purple. North of the house, the beds shimmer in white, pink, and silver. Such color play allows for seasonal variations; the garden stays fresh and the gardener stays inspired by changing bedding schemes each year by using annuals and temperennials. In summer, the beds on one side of the gothic "windows" are planted solely in the varying purples of bread seed poppies (*Papaver somniferum*) and allium; interest is created by the dark froth of interplanted bronze fennel, the different sizes and shapes of the alliums, and the note of blue introduced by the glaucous foliage of the poppies.